STERLING BIOGRAPHIES

HARRY HOUDINI

Death-Defying Showman

Rita Thievon Mullin

STERLING

New York / London
www.sterlingpublishing.com

Library of Congress Cataloging-in-Publication Data Available

10 9 8 7 6 5 4 3 2 1

Published by Sterling Publishing Co., Inc.
387 Park Avenue South, New York, NY 10016
© 2007 by Rita Thievon Mullin
Distributed in Canada by Sterling Publishing
c/o Canadian Manda Group, 165 Dufferin Street
Toronto, Ontario, Canada M6K 3H6
Distributed in the United Kingdom by GMC Distribution Services
Castle Place, 166 High Street, Lewes, East Sussex, England BN7 1XU
Distributed in Australia by Capricorn Link (Australia) Pty. Ltd.
P.O. Box 704, Windsor, NSW 2756, Australia

Printed in China
All rights reserved

Sterling ISBN-13: 978-1-4027-3262-1 (paperback)
         ISBN-10: 1-4027-3262-7
Sterling ISBN-13: 978-1-4027-4953-7 (hardcover)
         ISBN-10: 1-4027-4953-8

Designed by Joanna Ebenstein
Image research by Susan Schader

For information about custom editions, special sales, premium and
corporate purchases, please contact Sterling Special Sales
Department at 800-805-5489 or specialsales@sterlingpub.com.

Contents

Events in the Life of Harry Houdini

1874

March 24, 1874
Harry Houdini is born Ehrich Weiss in Budapest, Hungary, to Mayer and Cecelia Weiss.

September 1878
Cecelia Weiss and her sons move to Appleton, Wisconsin, to join her husband, who is serving as a rabbi.

Summer 1883
Ehrich performs as a trapeze artist in a neighborhood circus. Years later, Harry Houdini will mark this as the beginning of his career in show business.

1891
Ehrich Weiss and Jacob Hyman begin performing as professional magicians. They call themselves the Brothers Houdini. Ehrich changes his first name to Harry.

June 1894
Harry Houdini marries Bess Rahner only three weeks after meeting her in Coney Island, New York. She soon becomes his performing partner.

March 1899
Martin Beck hires Harry and Bess for the Orpheum vaudeville circuit.

July 1900
Harry and Bess open a successful run at the Alhambra Theater in London and soon begin a five-year record-breaking tour of Europe.

September 1906
The first issue of Houdini's *Conjurers' Monthly Magazine* is published. It ceases publication in 1908.

November 27, 1906
Houdini, in handcuffs, jumps into the Detroit River from the Belle Island Bridge.

1908
Houdini executes his milk can trick in public for the first time. It's the first underwater escape performed in a theater.

November 26, 1909
Houdini makes his first successful flight, in a Voisin biplane, outside Hamburg, Germany.

March 18, 1910
Houdini becomes the first person to fly on the continent of Australia.

July 1912
Houdini escapes from handcuffs and a sealed wooden box dumped into New York's East River.

September 21, 1912
Houdini performs the Upside Down escape in public for the first time.

July 17, 1913
Houdini's mother, Cecelia Weiss, dies.

1918
Houdini makes his first film, *The Master Mystery*. It features the first robot to appear in a popular movie.

April 14, 1920
Houdini visits Sir Arthur Conan Doyle, creator of Sherlock Holmes and a staunch believer in spiritualism.

Summer 1920
Houdini makes his first independent movie, *The Man from Beyond*, under the Houdini Picture Corporation; it closes down a few years later after the failure of its final movie, *Haldane*.

July 1924
As part of a panel of judges investigating psychic abilities, Houdini attends his first séance with medium Mina "Margery" Crandon.

August 5, 1926
Houdini remains underwater in a sealed casket for ninety minutes, winning an underwater challenge.

October 31, 1926
Houdini dies of an infection caused by a burst appendix.

1926

A Life Too Amazing for Fiction

What the eye[s] see and the ears hear, the mind believes.

Houdini. It sounds like the name of a comic-book superhero, daring and mysterious. But Houdini was real. His escapes were so fantastic that they seemed like fiction. But they really happened.

During his shows he would seem to do the impossible, overcoming every imaginable prison. He escaped from **handcuffs**, **straitjackets**, steel tanks, piano boxes, and even a coffin suspended underwater. Why, he seemed to be able to slip through cracks! As Houdini once said about his audience, "What the eye[s] see and the ears hear, the mind believes."

In a time when television was far in the future and even radio was still experimental, Houdini was one of the most famous names in the world. He was known from Appleton, Wisconsin, to Sydney, Australia. He was an escape artist, magician, airplane pioneer, movie star, and **debunker** of frauds. Today his name survives while the names of many of the most powerful people of his time have faded away. If his personality was larger than life, his life was more amazing than any story a novelist could imagine.

CHAPTER 1

Introducing Harry Houdini

I asked nothing more of life than to become in my profession like Robert-Houdin.

The mass of people in the streets of Washington, D.C., was, according to one newspaper, the largest "ever assembled in Washington at one place in the city except for the inauguration of a President." Harry Houdini, the most famous escape artist in the world, was hanging by his ankles and wrapped in a straitjacket hundreds of feet above them. The straitjacket completely restrained his upper body. But for Houdini it offered a perfect device for a dramatic escape.

Within only three minutes, he had pulled the jacket over his head and dropped it down to the crowd below. He extended his arms out to show that he was free of his **shackles**. The city echoed with the roar of the crowd as he was lowered back to the ground. The combination of physical strength and sheer daring needed to accomplish this feat left people breathless. No wonder people thought he was superhuman.

But Houdini was no superman. In fact, his early life was spent in poverty. He often wondered where his next meal would come from, but he had a large and loving family, and he loved them in return.

Throughout his life, Harry Houdini called Appleton, Wisconsin, his hometown. It was the first home he remembered, but it was not where he was born. He was

A crowd watches intently as Houdini escapes from a straitjacket while suspended from the roof of Keith's Theater in Washington, D.C., in 1922.

3

The first page of the Bible of Rabbi Samuel Weiss. He left Hungary in 1876 to find work with a congregation in America. His family, including son Ehrich, followed later.

born a world away in Europe, in Budapest, Hungary, on March 24, 1874. His original name was not Harry Houdini, either, but Ehrich Weiss.

Ehrich's father, Mayer Samuel Weiss, like many men in Europe at that time, went to America to find a better life for his family. Rabbi Weiss left Hungary to look for work as a rabbi, or Jewish holy man, when Ehrich was only two. Rabbi Weiss traveled to Appleton, where he knew some people who had arrived there earlier, and eventually found a Jewish congregation who asked him to lead them. Two years later, he had saved enough money for his wife, Cecelia, and their sons to follow him across the Atlantic Ocean.

Appleton was a beautiful small town surrounded by farms. It must have seemed like a paradise to four-year-old Ehrich and his brothers. Ehrich's mother, Cecelia, was a small, lively woman who cared for her children with her ready smile and a firm hand. She created a happy new home for her growing family. Their tiny apartment was filled with the aroma of potatoes and cabbages boiling for dinner as Mrs. Weiss mended worn pants and shirts to pass along to her younger children.

The family lived in an apartment over a shop on the main street, and the boys loved watching their neighbors come to town

Ehrich loved to attend the traveling circus and watch the trapeze artists, who flew through the air like the female acrobats depicted in this hand-colored lithograph c. 1890.

to shop, listening to the weekend band concerts in the park, and playing in the open fields nearby. Ehrich was most excited, though, when the traveling circus came to town each year. He was dazzled by the amazing feats of the **acrobats** as they spun and flew over the heads of the audience, and he came home dreaming of a life above the crowd. He hung a rope **trapeze** high in a tree and spent hours there each day, spinning around the trapeze bar until he had perfected his moves. But such a happy life was not to last.

In 1882, when Ehrich was eight, his father lost his job with his congregation. The family moved to Milwaukee, Wisconsin, a big city where his father hoped to find work. Ehrich missed

Even at eight years old, Ehrich worked and sold newspapers to help bring in money for the family.

Appleton very much. Times were tough for Ehrich's family, which now included seven children: Leo and Carrie Gladys were born while the family lived in Appleton, joining Herman, Nathan, William, Ehrich, and Theo.

Despite the family's move to the city, Mr. Weiss still had trouble finding jobs that paid enough to support his family. During their years in Milwaukee, they often moved to smaller, cheaper apartments.

Ehrich and his brothers all worked to bring extra money into the family. When he wasn't at school or practicing his circus tricks, he worked on street corners shining shoes and selling newspapers. He sold his first newspaper—*The Milwaukee Journal*—when he was only eight years old.

Working to Help the Family

The following year, one of his new friends decided to have a five-cent circus for the neighborhood children. Ehrich was thrilled. Dressed in long red stockings to resemble the tights he'd

A contortionist, like the one shown here in this undated photograph, is able to twist his body into amazing positions. Ehrich learned to become a contortionist, which was key to his later escape tricks.

seen the circus acrobats wear, he starred as a trapeze artist and **contortionist**, twisting his body into amazing shapes. He would use that skill throughout his life to escape from everything from straitjackets to giant milk cans. Years later, when Houdini held a celebration marking his thirty years in show business, he counted the time from 1883, when he was in that neighborhood children's circus.

When Ehrich was twelve, he really wanted to help support his family, but he could not find a steady job in Milwaukee. Hoping he would be able to find more work somewhere else, he made his first escape. He ran away from home. He hopped a train that he thought would take him to Texas but instead, it took him to Kansas City, Missouri. He wrote his mother a postcard so she would know he was safe, and he promised to return.

On another escape, he took his shoeshine kit to Delavan, a small town in Wisconsin that had an army base. Ehrich thought he could make a lot of money shining the soldiers' shoes. He did not realize the soldiers shined their own shoes. After a few days

In this postcard Ehrich sent to his mother when he ran away from home at age twelve to try to earn money for his struggling family, he tells her he will be home "in about a year."

When Ehrich was thirteen, he and his father moved to New York City, which was a vibrant city as seen in this photograph of Broadway c. 1900. It became Houdini's home for most of his life.

there without any food, he met a boy, Al Flitcroft, who lived on a farm nearby. The boy brought Ehrich back to his home, where his mother and father took Ehrich in, cleaned him up, fed him, and let him live with them while he looked for work.

Like many poor children of his time, Ehrich had to stop going to school so that he could work to help support his family. When he was thirteen, he and his father set off for New York City, where Rabbi Weiss hoped to have better luck finding a job. In New York, Ehrich truly found a new home. He continued to live there for the rest of his life. The city offered him many chances to earn money. He delivered messages and packages around town, made parts for machines, and cut fabric in a men's clothing factory.

The rest of the family followed a year later, after Ehrich and his father had saved enough for his mother and brothers and sister to join them. The family found a small apartment on East 75th Street. But life at home was still difficult. "We lived there, I mean starved there, several years," he later remembered. Then they moved to East 69th Street, where the family remained for many years.

Ehrich's brothers also found jobs to help support the family. Theo worked part-time with a photographer. The photographer enjoyed doing magic tricks in his spare time. One day Theo, who was two years younger than Ehrich, came rushing home to show his brother a disappearing coin trick the photographer had taught him. Ehrich studied what his brother was doing to make the coin disappear and reappear, and then he practiced it constantly. His smooth movements quickly made him better at the trick than Theo was, and soon he was amazing his friends with it.

Ehrich Weiss, age sixteen, wears medals he won as a member of the Pastime Athletic Club. He was a fierce competitor from childhood to his dying day.

Jean-Eugene Robert-Houdin

Jean-Eugene Robert-Houdin is known as the father of modern magic. He was the first to bring his magic act into theaters and the first to perform in modern, formal dress rather than wizard's robes. He perfected the "mind reading" tricks that earlier magicians had used. Wearing a blindfold, Robert-Houdin could identify objects belonging to audience members when his son held them up, giving his father secret verbal clues. Later, Houdini and his wife would make such tricks a part of their act.

This engraving shows Jean-Eugene Robert-Houdin with a chess-playing automaton, or robot, he built. He developed many mechanical gadgets for his magic act and for his own amusement.

A watchmaker by training, Robert-Houdin loved mechanical gadgets, and he made machines he called **automatons** that performed amazing tricks. He was the first magician to use electricity in his act. Using an electromagnet hidden beneath the stage, he could make a lightweight box lifted by an audience member become impossibly heavy when he commanded it—and his assistant turned on the electromagnet. The magnet attracted a metal bar inside the box, making it impossible for the audience member to pick it up when he tried again.

Jacob Hyman formed the Brothers Houdini with Ehrich Weiss when both were teenagers. By 1895, when this photo was taken, he had left the act but continued to perform escapes.

The Birth of Harry Houdini

When Ehrich was not working, he loved playing sports. He was a strong swimmer, an enthusiastic boxer, a bicycle racer, and a prize-winning runner. He especially loved to run over the broad, green fields of Central Park. As a member of the Pastime Athletic Club, Ehrich excelled at track, winning several first-place finishes as a runner. During the events, he wore red silk shorts that his mother sewed for him by hand.

Ehrich worked at H. Richters' Sons necktie factory for more than two years while he was a teenager. He cut fabric that would be made into men's ties, but he learned a great deal more than how to handle scissors. During his breaks at the factory, he would practice magic tricks and exchange secrets with Jacob Hyman, his best friend and another aspiring magician. The two friends began performing their magic act around town, wearing costumes sewn by Ehrich's mother. Soon they decided to try to become professionals, but they needed a name for their act.

Ehrich read every book he could find about magic tricks and techniques. One of the books that he read would change his life—and his name. It was the autobiography of Jean-Eugene Robert-Houdin, the father of modern magic. "From the moment I began to study the art he became my guide and my hero," Houdini wrote later. "I asked nothing more of life than to become in my profession like Robert-Houdin." Becoming like him in name was easy. Adding an "i" to the end of a name was a popular way to pay tribute to earlier magicians. The boys became the Brothers Houdini. And Ehrich, who was often called "Ehrie," became "Harry." So Harry Houdini was born.

Ehrich read every book he could find about magic tricks and techniques.

CHAPTER 2

The Houdinis

When I clap my hands three times—behold a miracle!

When Ehrich Weiss and Jacob Hyman, his friend from the tie-cutting factory, set out to make their fortune as the Brothers Houdini in 1891, they could not have guessed how difficult it would be. The Brothers Houdini performed on street corners and at one-night engagements when they could find them. They did card tricks, pulled silk handkerchiefs from flames, and made flowers appear from buttonholes. These were all tricks that did not require expensive equipment, just plenty of practice and showmanship. And practice and study they did. Harry read every book he could find that would help him develop his skills as a magician.

One of the best sources he found was a book about spiritualism, not magic. Spiritualism was a movement that claimed dead people lived in a spirit world and that only select people, called **mediums**, were able to speak to them. In meetings called **séances**, mediums said they could receive communications in the form of knocking or other sounds. One of the books Harry read was called *Revelations of a Spirit Medium*. It outlined the tricks these mediums used to fool people into believing they were actually receiving signals from the dead.

To show they were not making the sounds themselves, mediums would sometimes be tied to their

The title page from Houdini's copy of *Revelations of a Spirit Medium* shows a drawing of a medium pretending to speak with the dead. Houdini learned many escape skills from the book.

chairs. Harry studied the tricks mediums used to secretly slip from knotted ropes that tied their hands and feet. He practiced his rope escapes by the hour, even learning to free himself from a large canvas sack pulled tight with drawstrings and knotted. He learned more rope tricks from George Dexter, one of the men who announced the acts at Huber's Museum in New York, where the boys sometimes performed. Dexter had spent his life in show business and was a master of rope escapes. He even taught Harry some secrets for escaping from handcuffs.

In 1892, Rabbi Weiss died, and Mrs. Weiss had to look to her sons to care for the family. Ehrich, who was now known as Harry to everyone but his mother, gave his mother a large portion of what little money he made as a magician. Two years later, his friend Jacob decided he had had enough of trying to make a living from magic and sold his interest in the Brothers Houdini to Harry. Soon Harry's brother Theo became his partner. For the first time, the Brothers Houdini really were brothers!

Metamorphosis

Around this time, Harry used some of the money he had saved to buy a piece of equipment that someday would help to make him a star. It was a box. But it was not an ordinary box. The box was the size of the trunks people used to pack their belongings for long sea voyages. But unlike those trunks, this box had a secret panel that allowed hidden objects to be removed from inside secretly.

The box trick worked like this: Theo had his hands tied behind his back and was put into a large sack that was tied closed. The sack, with Theo inside, was locked in the box, and the box was wrapped with ropes to make it extra secure. Then a tall frame with curtains on it was put around the box so that the audience could not see inside. Once the curtains were in place, Harry would say, "When I clap my hands three times—behold a miracle!" and slip behind the curtains. In a matter of a few seconds, Theo would walk through the curtains and Harry would be gone. When the box was reopened, there was Harry, inside the sack in the locked box, with his hands tied behind his back. They called

Theo, shown here at age twenty-one, joined his brother Harry several years before to become "The Brothers Houdini."

> *The change was as dramatic as the metamorphosis of a caterpillar into a butterfly in nature.*

the quick-change trick "Metamorphosis." The change was as dramatic as the **metamorphosis** of a caterpillar into a butterfly in nature.

During one show at the Imperial Theater in New York, Harry clapped his hands three times and slipped behind the curtain. The audience waited. And waited. And waited some more. Nothing happened. Behind the curtain Harry desperately untied and unlocked the box. Theo had left the key to the secret panel in the dressing room and could not get out! The Brothers Houdini were not invited back to perform at the Imperial Theater the next day. And Harry made certain that only he would be locked inside the box in the future. He would not let the success of his act depend on his brother's poor memory.

Love at First Sight

In spring of 1894, when Harry was twenty, he and Theo were performing at Coney Island, a popular beach town outside of New York City. One evening, Theo asked Harry to join him after the show to meet

Beatrice Rahner is photographed in 1894, the year she married Harry Houdini. Bess, as she was called, left the Floral Sisters act to join her new husband as his performing partner.

the Floral Sisters, two young women who did a song and dance act. When Harry agreed to come along that evening, he could not have known his life would change forever. Bess Rahner, one of the Floral Sisters, and Harry Houdini knew from the moment they met that they were meant for each other. A tiny woman, barely five feet, Bess made the five-foot-five-inch Harry look tall. And she was taken by his charm, determination, and handsome smile. In Bess, Harry saw not only the love of his life but a perfect partner.

A poster promoting the "only and original" Houdinis celebrated the Metamorphosis, the three-second-change act that first made them famous. The poster was created in 1895, the year after they married.

Over the next three weeks, they spent all their free time together and were secretly married. Later they were married by a priest and by a rabbi since Bess was Catholic and Harry was Jewish. Bess later joked, "I'm the most married woman I know. I've been married three times, and all to the same man."

With Bess on the scene, Theo left the act, and the Brothers Houdini now simply became the Houdinis. Tiny and nimble Bess learned to slip inside the Metamorphosis box quickly, and the switch was made in the blink of an eye. For years, the trick was the highlight of their act.

That fall, Harry and Bess headed out on the road when they could get a booking in a dime museum or beer garden. Dime museums featured giants or bearded women, and short

Dime Museums and Beer Gardens

For the price of a few cents, poor families living in cities could be entertained by magicians and contortionists and could gawk at natural and man-made curiosities in dime museums. The Houdini Brothers performed at Huber's Museum, New York's oldest dime museum, on a simple stage wedged between collections of unusual objects meant to amaze and educate. The visitors would stop to watch a performer as they wandered through the collections of unusual minerals, exotic stuffed and live animals, human **anomalies**, and tools for testing their own strength and health.

Beer gardens offered poor immigrants from Eastern Europe a taste of home. These outdoor gathering places offered inexpensive beer, lots of laughter and conversation, and occasional programs with magicians, singers, and other performers.

This promotional announcement, from the Houdinis' days in dime museums, praises the "expert handcuff manipulator." His escapes were soon being noticed—and imitated—by others.

performances by magicians, singers, or comedians. Sometimes they were in a city for only a day or two. If they were lucky, they might stay in one place for two or three weeks. The work was hard. They would perform from morning until night, sometimes doing as many as twenty shows on a weekend day.

For all their work, the Houdinis received only $20 a week, and Bess cooked what little food they could afford on a small alcohol stove in cheap rented rooms. Nearly starving on the road, they returned to New York and spent the winter living in Mrs. Weiss's crowded apartment.

In the spring of 1895, the Houdinis signed on for a season with the Welsh Brothers Circus. They were not only paid, but they had a free place to sleep and all the food they could eat. Their time with the circus was hectic but happy. They made friends with the many performers and learned new skills. One artist, a member of the San Kitchy Akimoto troupe, a Japanese acrobatic act, could swallow an ivory ball and then **regurgitate** it into his mouth. Harry was fascinated! The man showed Harry his secret, and Harry practiced this trick using a small, peeled potato attached to a string. The string allowed him to pull it back up if it got stuck in

Harry and Bess Houdini worked with the Welsh Brothers Circus in 1895. They are seated in the front row, right. Harry did card tricks, performed magic, and even worked the puppets.

Traveling Circuses

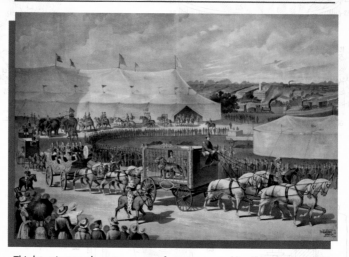

This late nineteenth-century poster featuring a caged lion, elephants, and camels promotes a traveling circus. Circus performers would parade through towns to gather crowds for the show.

The late nineteenth century, when Houdini was a boy, was the golden age of circuses. These traveling shows were the only form of entertainment for most people living in small towns sprinkled across America. Contortionists, clowns, wild animals, acrobats, trapeze artists, and magicians dazzled youngsters and instilled in them dreams of life under the big top—the tent under which the larger circuses performed.

The first circus came to America from England in 1793. Soon, an elephant was added to one show, and the age of circus animals had begun. By the 1820s, thirty or more traveling shows included wild animals. The circus crew would pitch their tent and perform for a day or two, then pack up their wagons and ride through the night to a nearby town a few miles away.

his throat, and if he swallowed it completely, his teacher told him, no harm would be done. He would simply digest it. Soon Harry was "swallowing" ivory balls. This skill would someday come in handy for hiding keys when he was a master escape artist.

On the Road

By the end of the circus season, Harry and Bess had saved enough money to invest in a struggling traveling show called the American Gaiety Girls. As one of the new owners, Harry was anxious to bring in lots of paying customers. During his circus days, he had begun collecting different kinds of handcuffs. While traveling with the American Gaiety Girls he first came up with the idea of having himself handcuffed during Metamorphosis rather than simply having his hands tied with rope. It was the first time he escaped from handcuffs on stage.

During this time he also showed his amazing talent for promoting his act. He visited the police station in Gloucester, Massachusetts, before the company's first performance there. He challenged them to put him into their best handcuffs, old or new. In minutes he escaped from every set that the police officers had. While promoting their show in Woonsocket, Rhode Island, he invited a local newspaper reporter to the police station, who watched as Houdini quickly escaped from six sets of handcuffs at the same time. A story praising him for his escapes appeared in the next day's newspaper.

Despite Harry and Bess's best efforts, the American Gaiety Girls show failed. Over the next several years, Harry and Bess moved from one company to another, performing in small towns throughout the country. Those years on the road were the best school a performer could have. They polished their act and learned how to promote themselves by using reporters, policemen, politicians, and stunts to attract audiences.

After performing in dime museums and with traveling companies that kept going out of business, Harry and Bess returned to the Welsh Brothers Circus in 1898. Their Metamorphosis act was so successful that by the end of the season it had become the show's big final act.

In the fall of 1898, Harry and Bess returned home after the circus closed for the season. By then, Harry had been performing for seven years, but the kind of stardom he dreamed of seemed as far away as ever. He decided that he would give himself one more year to make it big. If he failed, he said he would retire and find a "real job." Bess's brother-in-law offered to help Harry get a job with Yale, a big lock-making company. Harry never had to accept the offer. His big break was only a few months away.

Draped in chains, handcuffs, and locks, Houdini poses for a promotional photo around 1899. By then, he was making a name for himself with his dramatic escapes.

CHAPTER 3

The Handcuff King

Why don't you cut out the magical stuff and just give a couple of big thrillers, like the handcuffs and the trunk trick?

—Martin Beck

In late 1898, Harry and Bess headed out to perform throughout the Midwest. They thought these would be their last performances before they would return home to a life of steady jobs and home-cooked meals. If it was to be their final show-business tour, then Harry was determined to go out with a bang.

When they arrived in Chicago, he wanted to promote the act by challenging local police to lock him in their toughest handcuffs inside their strongest jail cell. But Chicago was a big city, and unlike the police in small towns, the city police were not as interested in helping a small-time performer get some press. He looked up Detective-Lieutenant Andy Rohan, a police officer and important man in the city, hoping that by becoming friendly with him they could make a splash. While Bess chatted with Rohan, Harry slipped back into the jail cell area to study the locks.

Harry returned the next day with some reporter friends and asked to be locked into a cell so that he could try to escape. They locked him in a cell and returned to Rohan's office to chat while Houdini struggled. When Harry joined the reporters and policemen only a few minutes later, no one was impressed. They all thought he had made a copy of a cell key when he had been there before and had hidden it in his clothes. Harry was outraged that they would think he would stoop to such a cheap trick. He had to think quickly about his next response.

"Suppose you strip me and search me before you lock me up?" he said.

So they stripped him of all his clothes, put him in handcuffs and leg irons, and even sealed his mouth shut in case he was hiding a key there. Then they locked him in a cell and left his clothes in another cell. Ten minutes later he was back, dressed and carrying the cuffs and leg irons. Even the big-city police and reporters were impressed this time. An article appeared in the next day's newspaper praising his amazing trick. Harry was thrilled. He sent copies to every agent and theater manager he knew. The publicity paid off. Harry and Bess were hired to perform for several days at the city's famous Hopkins Theater.

After their successful run in Chicago, Harry and Bess returned to playing in small dime museums. They appeared with such acts as "the tiniest triplets ever born," tattooed women, English ballad

The dime museums of Houdini's time featured many acts, such as comedians, snake handlers, and tattooed people similar to the woman shown in this photograph from 1907.

Crowds walk past two vaudeville theaters in New York in 1905. The family-friendly fare made vaudeville popular for rich and poor patrons.

singers, Irish comedians and "Thardo, the rattlesnake poison **defier**." Many of the people they performed with during those early days taught Harry secrets he would use later in his act, and they remained lifelong friends of Harry and Bess.

The Big Break

While Harry and Bess were performing at the Palmgarden, a beer hall in Minneapolis, Minnesota, in early 1899, a group of men was passing through, scouting for new performers for their vaudeville theaters. Vaudeville was the name for variety shows performed in comfortable theaters rather than noisy, dingy beer halls or dime museums. Proper ladies and their families did not visit dime museums. Harry and Bess had long dreamed of stardom on the vaudeville circuit—a network of theaters around

Vaudeville

In the 1880s, theaters began offering variety shows that featured a broad range of talents—from opera singers to comedians and tap dancers and **novelty acts**. These programs, usually made up of eight to ten acts, were appropriate for families, and drew audiences from the poor to the rich. Vaudeville theaters in big cities such as Boston, Chicago, and New York were huge and very ornate.

Many popular radio, movie, and television stars got their start in vaudeville. In the 1920s, Judy Garland (left) sang with her sisters in a vaudeville act known as the Gumm Sisters. She would later star as Dorothy in the movie *The Wizard of Oz*.

The name vaudeville may have come from the French term *vaux-de-vire*, referring to **satirical** songs sung to popular tunes in the 1400s. The exotic name probably made people believe they were seeing something cultural—and having fun at the same time.

Performers traveled over a circuit of theaters around the country, staying in a city for anywhere from a day or two to a few weeks. Animal acts, tap dancers, magicians, escape artists, singers, dance troupes, and comedians were usually included on a bill, each performing for ten to fifteen minutes several times a day.

When motion pictures became popular, short films were shown at the end of programs. But soon the movies became more popular than the live acts. By the 1920s, when movies had sound, the live acts were fading from the bill. Many famous vaudeville performers became movie, radio, and television stars, such as Judy Garland (who was one of the Gumm Sisters), George Burns, Jack Benny, Bob Hope, and W.C. Fields.

the country. The programs had singers, dancers, comedians, magicians, and other performers whose acts were enjoyed by the whole family. Vaudeville theaters had become very popular in large- and medium-sized cities. The audiences were friendly, the pay was good, and a performer might sign on for forty weeks traveling from one city to the next on a circuit tour.

One evening when Harry and Bess had finished their act at the beer hall, a well-dressed gentleman invited them to join him at a nearby restaurant. They were tired and hungry and happy for the invitation. Bess later remembered that once they sat down, Harry asked the man how he had liked the act.

"I think you're a rotten showman," the man replied. "Why don't you cut out the magical stuff and just give a couple of big thrillers, like the handcuffs and the trunk trick?"

Harry and Bess were stunned.

"You have two big stunts at which nobody else can touch you. Those are the things to cash in on. I'll try you out on the circuit at sixty

Houdini, the "world's handcuff king and jail-breaker," tops the bill in this poster for the Orpheum Theatre vaudeville show around the turn of the twentieth century.

Houdini had one of the largest hand-cuff collections in America during his lifetime. Displayed are some of Houdini's handcuffs and leg irons (bottom) from the Outagamie Museum in Wisconsin.

dollars, and if you make it go, I'll raise you. My name is Martin Beck."

Martin Beck was one of the most important men in vaudeville. He managed the Orpheum theaters that stretched throughout the West and Midwest. He booked them at a theater in Omaha, Nebraska. If that went well, he said, he would give them a raise and send them to more theaters around the country.

Sixty dollars a week was more money than they had ever earned in their lives. They opened in Omaha in April with an act made up of handcuff challenges, leg iron escapes, and the Metamorphosis box trick.

Others had performed handcuff escapes before. But none of them had dared to let the audience bring their own cuffs to challenge them. To ensure he always could win those challenges, Harry became a serious student of locks. He talked to **locksmiths** in every city and studied books and pamphlets to learn how every kind of handcuff and leg iron worked.

He had already learned that all cuffs made by one company could be opened with a single key. Handcuffs had been around for a long time, though, and there were many different types of cuffs. When an audience member brought handcuffs onstage that Harry did not know, he would ask if he could keep them as a souvenir if he was able to get out of them. Most customers were happy to agree, so his handcuff collection soon became enormous.

Harry always insisted that cuffs be locked and unlocked with a key before he would be locked in. He had learned from experience that some people might play dirty tricks. During a performance in Evanston, Illinois, months before, a policeman had put him in cuffs from which Harry could not escape. Harry was frustrated during his act and furious afterward when he learned that the policeman had jammed the locks so that they could not be opened. Houdini had to be cut out of them.

Martin Beck raised Harry and Bess's salary to $90 a week and sent them on to San Francisco, the first stop on a tour of the West Coast.

After he was properly handcuffed and in leg irons, he would enter a four-sided "cabinet" of curtains to work in secret as a band played dramatic music that got faster and faster with each passing moment. He quickly learned to make even easy escapes look difficult so that the audience would be impressed by all his efforts.

Audiences in Omaha loved Harry. Martin Beck raised Harry and Bess's salary to $90 a week and sent them on to San Francisco, the first stop on a tour of the West Coast. By the time Harry left San Francisco, Martin Beck was paying him $150 a week. To celebrate, Harry bought Bess a small fur that wrapped around her neck. It was the height of fashion and nicer than anything she had ever owned before. He also began sending his mother more money each week. They traveled throughout the West, performing in theaters in Los Angeles, California;

Memphis and Nashville, Tennessee and Kansas City, Missouri, through the fall of 1899.

New Tricks in the Act

Harry Houdini was always seeking new ways to surprise and impress his audiences. During his first year traveling on the Orpheum circuit, he added several amazing new routines to his act. In the spring, he began performing the needle-swallowing act, a trick he had learned from a Hindu **conjurer** a few years before at the 1893

Bess and Harry Houdini pose for a portrait five years after their marriage. Their partnership continued onstage and off until Houdini's death.

World's Fair in Chicago. With audience members onstage to watch him closely, Harry would put as many as twenty-five sewing needles in his mouth and begin chewing—loudly. After he opened his mouth to show that the needles were gone, he would begin swallowing a long piece of thread. When only a small piece was left in his mouth, he would slowly pull it back out. As the thread emerged from his mouth, the needles were whole and all attached to it!

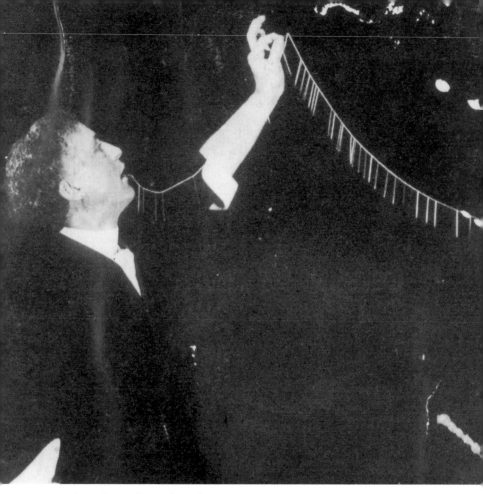

Houdini performing his needle-swallowing act in 1924. He introduced the trick into his show around 1900, years after he learned it from another performer.

Escapes were always the hit of his performance. He escaped from thumb cuffs, cuffs with time locks, even leg irons made during the Civil War. Remembering the straitjacket he had seen and practiced with after a tour of a **psychiatric** hospital in Canada the year before, he asked the head of the local hospital to put him into a straitjacket as part of a demonstration in San

Francisco. He escaped in minutes and soon made straitjacket escapes part of his publicity tours of cities.

By early 1900, jail cell escapes had become an important part of the promotion for Harry's performances. In Kansas City, detectives searched him, locked him in four pairs of handcuffs, placed shackles on his ankles and chains connecting his arms and legs, and put him in a cell with a new lock that required two keys to open. They threw a sheet over the cell so he could work in private, and seven minutes later he was free of the shackles and was walking out of the cell.

He escaped in minutes and soon made straitjacket escapes part of his publicity tours of cities.

By this time, Harry Houdini was making $400 each week, an amount many families of that time managed to live on for a year. He had conquered the great theaters in America's West. But the more sophisticated audiences in New York and other eastern cities seemed to prefer acts that came from Europe. So in May 1900, Harry and Bess boarded the SS *Kensington* and sailed to England, determined to conquer Europe so that they could conquer the rest of America.

CHAPTER 4

Taking the Stage in Europe

I make the most money, I think, in Russia and Paris, for the people of those countries are so willing to be amused, so eager to see something new and out of the ordinary.

Harry and Bess set sail for England in 1900 with no promises of bookings and only enough money to last them for a week at an actors' boardinghouse in London. To keep busy, Harry entertained the other passengers with magic tricks. One of them wrote him a letter of introduction to C. Dundas Slater, who managed London's Alhambra Theater, one of Great Britain's finest. Harry presented Slater with a homemade scrapbook collection of all of Harry's newspaper clippings. But Slater was still skeptical, so he let Harry give a "private performance" to a small group of newspaper reporters and Scotland Yard officers. Harry knew it was really an audition, so he gave it his all. He wowed them. Slater immediately signed Harry to a two-week run at the Alhambra beginning in July.

This publicity sheet from around 1900 promotes Houdini's great success in London at the Alhambra Theater. Houdini loved to get endorsements for his escape act from policemen, as shown here.

Escape from the Bean Giant

As Houdini stepped onstage on opening night, a man came running down the aisle accusing Houdini of being an **imposter**. He was not even an American, the man claimed. Houdini's accuser was a man named Cirnoc, who claimed to be "The Original King of Handcuffs." Before Harry could respond, another man stood up in Harry's defense and said he was an American lawyer who had seen Houdini perform in the United States. The audience hooted at Cirnoc.

Harry knew he had to take Cirnoc on. "Get me the Bean Giant," he whispered to Bess. The Bean Giant was a huge handcuff invented by a Captain Bean. It was so large, in fact, that a person locked into it could not reach the keyhole even if he had a key. Houdini was the only person who had been able to release himself from it, and Captain Bean himself had given him a set.

Harry offered Cirnoc $500 if he could escape from them. Cirnoc wanted to see Houdini get out of them first.

"Lock me in," was Harry's reply.

He stepped into his curtained cabinet and returned a few moments later carrying the Bean Giant.

Houdini then locked Cirnoc into the cuffs and even gave

The Bean Giant was one of Houdini's favorite handcuff designs. Patented in 1887, it was one of the most unusual handcuffs of Houdini's time and difficult to escape from—even with a key.

"The Original King of Handcuffs" the key. As the audience whistled and mocked him, Cirnoc struggled, twisting and turning as he tried to get the key into the keyhole. He finally had to give up and ask Harry to release him. Cirnoc shook Harry's hand before he sheepishly left the stage.

Harry was so successful that his run was then extended through the end of August, when he was scheduled to appear in Dresden, Germany. During his summer in London, Harry spent his spare time studying every kind of handcuff and lock used in Europe. He knew that his handcuff challenge, which had worked so well in the U.S., could open him up to some nasty surprises, since he would be challenged by many different types of cuffs and locks as he traveled from country to country. His hard work and study paid off. Throughout all the countries of Europe where he appeared during the next five years, he was never defeated in his handcuff challenge.

Triumph in Germany

In September 1900, Harry and Bess headed to Germany, where they were scheduled to appear at Dresden's Central Theater. On opening night, the Central Theater owner, Gustav Kammsetzer, told Houdini that if the audience whistled, the equivalent to American "boos," Houdini's first night in Dresden would be his last.

After Harry's first handcuff escape, the audience members jumped to their feet, applauding. "And above all the din and noise and shouts and screams of the public," Harry wrote to a friend back home, he could hear Kammsetzer "shouting like a madman. He ran to the middle of the stage and applauded. He took off his hat and he cheered." Harry's run at the Central Theater broke all box-office records.

OUDINI ist in Amerika aus 4 Gefängnissen, New-York, Kansas City, Buffalo und Chicago ausgebrochen, worüber jederzeit Atteste zur Verfügung stehen.

Die Polizei in Kansas City stellte HOUDINI folgendes Attest aus:

Den deutschen Polizei-Behörden stehen HOUDINI nachfolgende Original-Atteste zur Verfügung.

| Königl. Polizei-Präsidium Berlin. | Königl. Sächs. Polizei-Direction | Das Polizeiamt der Stadt Leipzig. | Der Königl. Polizei-Präsident |

Windheim
Königl. Ober-Regierungs-Rath.

Koettig
Ober-Regierungs-Rath.

Müller.

Finger.

Außerdem besitzt HARRY HOUDINI weitere Original-Atteste der hohen Polizei England's und Amerika's.

A schedule shows a listing of Houdini's performances in Germany in 1900. His triumph there made him a European star. He toured Europe for five years before returning to American stages.

Harry Houdini was in demand. Kammsetzer begged the manager of the Wintergarten Theater in Berlin to delay Houdini's opening there by a month so that he could extend the run in Dresden. The manager refused. Harry opened in Berlin in October and stayed until the end of November, when he returned to the Alhambra Theater in London.

With Harry's great success in England and Germany came many more handcuff escape artists. If imitators were going to make money off his name, he thought, he should at least keep it in the family. "Come over, the apples are ripe," he cabled to his brother Theo in New York and sent him money to sail to Europe. Theo, who had been his partner in the Brothers Houdini before Harry married Bess, was then performing magic and escapes in the U.S. He caught the first ship he could get. By the time he arrived, Theo later recalled, Harry "had my act framed—settings, handcuffs, a substitution trunk, a girl assistant—even bookings in opposition to his own. He had even picked out the name by which I was to be known." From then on Theo was called "Hardeen."

Harry continued his successful tour of Germany. By May 1901, only a year after he had left for Europe without any

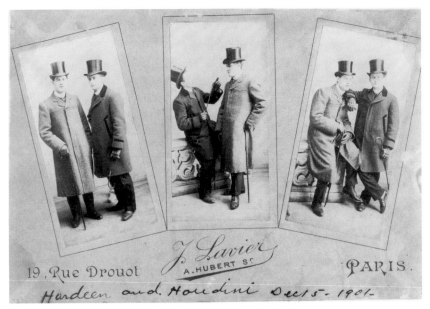

19, Rue Drouot   A. HUBERT Sr   PARIS.

Hardeen and Houdini Dec 15 - 1901

Harry Houdini and his brother Theo—now known as Hardeen—pose for photos in Europe in 1901. The two toured separately throughout the continent, performing escapes and sharing techniques.

engagements and nearly broke, he had become Germany's most popular vaudeville performer.

Traveling Around Europe

In November 1901, Houdini made his first trip to Paris, where he was signed to a two-month contract as the headliner at the Olympia Theater. Houdini was always looking for clever ways to promote his shows. While in Paris, he hired seven bald men and had them sit beside each other in sidewalk cafés around the city, all dressed the same and wearing bowler hats. Every few minutes they would remove their hats and lower their heads toward the traffic. Each man had a large, single letter on the top of his head. Together they spelled "HOUDINI."

Houdini Imitators

As Houdini became more famous, imitators started popping up all over Europe. "If you throw a stone in the air it will fall down and hit someone who has a handcuff key in his pocket and a 'Handcuff King' idea in his head," Houdini complained while touring England. They even copied his name: Hourdene, Whodini, Cutini, and Stillini all tried to benefit from Houdini's popularity.

Harry decided to take advantage of the Houdini hunger. In addition to setting up his brother Theo, who performed as Hardeen, as a competitor, he later trained a young woman to escape from a straitjacket and to perform some of his other famous routines. The posters for her act had Houdini's name in large type. Beneath it was the explanation that his escapes would be performed by "Miss Trixie."

While in Paris, he traveled to the grave side of Jean-Eugene Robert-Houdin, his hero and namesake. Throughout his tour of Europe, he bought hundreds of books about the history of magic, and he tried to meet any surviving experts of the previous century. He also collected posters and **playbills** of the great magicians, a collection that grew to enormous size in his lifetime.

During the four years Harry and Bess traveled around Europe performing for larger and larger audiences, they were lugging around more and more equipment. They needed help. Harry found the perfect assistant in Germany. His name was Franz Kukol. He was tall, had a big mustache, and spoke several languages. He joined Harry and Bess in 1903 to assist them in making arrangements, setting up the act in theaters, rehearsing the music with theater orchestras, and sometimes filling in for

Bess onstage. Before he could join, though, he had to sign a document swearing him to secrecy about Houdini's methods. He remained with Houdini until he left the act during World War I. He even named his son Harry Houdini Kukol.

Adding New Elements to the Act

When Harry performed his handcuff escapes from inside his drapery cabinet in Europe's large theaters, some people claimed he could have had help coming up to him through trap doors in the stage. The old dime museums and beer halls where Harry used to perform never had anything so grand as trap doors, so no one before had imagined he could have had anyone helping him inside the cabinet. To prove to audiences that no one was back there helping him, Harry and Franz developed a shorter frame behind which Harry would kneel to remove the handcuffs. The drapes were so low that the audience could see his face as he struggled but not his hands. As

The burial marker of Jean-Eugene Robert-Houdin, the father of modern magic and Houdini's youthful inspiration. Houdini visited the grave site of Robert-Houdin and many other famous magicians during his European tours.

Houdini was not just a master showman; he was also a great promoter. While performing in New York City, he arranged for a pair of goats to pull a wagon that carried a sign advertising his performance as the Handcuff King. The photo was probably taken by his loyal assistant Franz Kukol.

he escaped from each cuff, he would slide it across the stage. The audiences loved the suspense as they watched him sweat and turn red while forcing the chains and cuffs.

As Harry continued to welcome handcuff challenges, he added a new element: the box challenge. In city after city, local carpenters would build more and more elaborate packing boxes from which the great Houdini would escape. Often the box would be displayed in the theater lobby for days before a big performance so that audiences could see how sturdy it was.

After the box was carried on stage, Houdini would be

Franz Kukol

Franz Kukol became Harry Houdini's first assistant in 1903. A former Austrian army officer, Kukol made certain that arrangements for Houdini's travel and act were perfectly planned. He was a good mechanic, which helped when he and Houdini worked on new escapes. He was also a musician. He arranged music that entertained audiences and often masked tell-tale noises from behind the curtain as Houdini escaped from assorted onstage prisons.

Kukol also appeared on stage when needed, handing Houdini handcuffs and other equipment. Next to Bess, Kukol was Houdini's most important assistant and professional **confidant**. In 1913 in London, Houdini called the surprised Kukol out onstage in the middle of the performance to give him an engraved gold pocket watch marking their ten years together. The applause this time was not for Houdini, but for Franz Kukol. Although Kukol stopped working for Houdini during World War I and Houdini was to have several other loyal assistants over the years, none was more devoted than Kukol.

handcuffed, chained, and lifted into the box. The carpenters would put the top on the box and seal it shut with plenty of nails. Then the tall drapery cabinet would be placed around it to hide what was happening inside from the audience. The theater band played faster and louder with each passing minute, as Houdini worked to escape first from his bonds and then from the box. When he emerged from the cabinet and the drapery was opened, the box stood there, just as it had, with all the sides—and all the nails that had sealed it—still in place.

So amazing were his feats that some people in Europe claimed Houdini had supernatural powers. Houdini was always quick to say that his skills were all based in the natural world. In the case of his many box escapes, the trick was simple: Before the performance Harry and Franz would replace the long nails holding one side of the box with shorter nails that Harry could easily push out from the inside. Then, once Houdini was out, he could tap the long ones back in while the band played louder and faster.

As the box challenge became more popular, Houdini developed new ways to amaze audiences. Sometimes the box was actually built onstage in front of the audience, so substituting short "**dummy** nails" was impossible. In that case, Houdini might use a simple steel jack that worked like the ones used to raise a

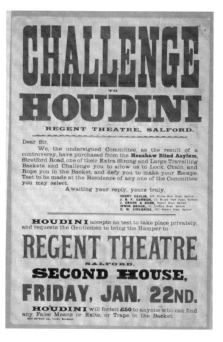

A committee challenges Houdini to escape from one of their "Extra Strong and Large Travelling Baskets" in this performance poster. When Houdini began featuring challenge escapes, audiences became extremely creative.

car for changing a tire. He would hide the parts of the jack in his clothing and assemble them after he was sealed in the box. The jack would apply pressure to one side of the box until the nails slipped out. After he was outside, he would take the jack apart again, hide the parts, and tap the nails back in place while the house band played the ear-blasting "Storm King" for the audience to hide the noise.

During the nearly five years Harry and Bess traveled throughout Europe, they became the most popular vaudeville performers there.

During the nearly five years Harry and Bess traveled throughout Europe, they became the most popular vaudeville performers there. They played to packed houses and received reviews in newspapers that any performer would envy. Although they had made two trips back to the U.S. to visit family during their time in Europe, by 1905 they were homesick and ready to move back to take on American vaudeville, if the offers were good enough. The best was yet to come.

CHAPTER 5

Daring New Escapes

[The crowd reached] a pitch of excitement bordering on hysteria.
— Reporter at a Houdini performance

When Harry and Bess returned home to New York in the summer of 1905, they spent a few months relaxing in the big house they had bought in New York City. The house at 278 West 113th Street was huge, with a dozen rooms on four floors. It had plenty of space for Harry's growing collection of books and memorabilia on the history of magic. It also had room for his mother, sister, and two of his brothers. They lived there in style whether Harry and Bess were in town or on the road. His mother was getting older, and each time Harry parted from her for Europe, he worried that it might be for the last time. An American tour would keep him closer to his mother.

Harry and Bess headed out on an American tour that fall. As the act had

Houdini with his two "sweethearts," his mother, Cecelia Steiner Weiss (left), and his wife, Beatrice "Bess" Houdini (right). He was a devoted son and husband throughout his life.

changed from magic to escape, Bess's role had shifted from onstage assistant to offstage partner. She made certain Harry remembered to eat when he was deeply involved in doing research or designing a new routine, she gave him moral support and a sympathetic ear, and she managed many of the details of their travel schedule. They seldom performed the old Metamorphosis trick anymore, so Bess was rarely onstage with Harry, but she was as important to his success as she had ever been. She was his keeper of secrets and his most important supporter. Harry and Bess never had any children. They loved and cared for many pets over the years—even teaching them handcuff tricks.

All Challengers Welcome

On the new tour, Harry expanded the box challenge that had been so popular in Europe. This time, he invited people to dare him to escape from just about anything. The challengers were very creative! During his tour he escaped from the world's largest envelope (without tearing the paper), a clear-glass box, a coffin with the top screwed down, a man-sized sausage skin, and a giant-sized football carried onstage by the University of Pennsylvania football team. In each case, he was also handcuffed and chained before being sealed inside. Audiences were enthusiastic, to say the least. In one city, a reporter said the crowd reached "a pitch of excitement bordering on hysteria." The tour was so successful that Harry's theater contract was renewed for another thirty-five weeks, keeping the Houdinis on the road for three years.

One of Houdini's most astonishing escapes happened in Boston in February 1906. Workers from the Riverside Boiler Works challenged him to escape from an iron hot-water tank five feet high and two feet across. The tank was placed on its side

Bess and Harry's Pets

In their early days on the road, Harry and Bess's act included white birds named Lord and Lady Snowball who lived with them in their rooms. In later years, they had many birds at their house in New York, including parrots they had trained to talk and imitate sounds.

For years they took their little white dog, Charlie, with them on tour, sometimes using Houdini's **sleight of hand** to hide him from border guards as they crossed into new countries in Europe.

In 1918, they got a new dog they named Bobby Houdini. Houdini fashioned miniature "paw cuffs" and taught Bobby how to escape from them. He brought Bobby to the annual dinner of the Society of American Magicians to perform as "the Only Handcuff King Dog in the World."

onstage, with only its top open. Handcuffed and chained, Harry crawled inside. Then the men riveted the opening, inserting bolts into it and bending the ends of the bolts to create two heads. These could only be removed by sawing the bolts apart.

The curtain cabinet was then brought out to hide the tank. As the music began, the audience waited, certain Houdini had met his match. An hour after the committee had riveted him into the tank, Houdini finally opened the curtains and stumbled out, his suit torn and dirty. The audience's cheers were deafening. The committee was astounded. They investigated the tank to see whether all the rivets were in place. They were. Then they wondered whether they had been tricked into sealing a Houdini double inside. They cut off the bolts to check. The tank was empty.

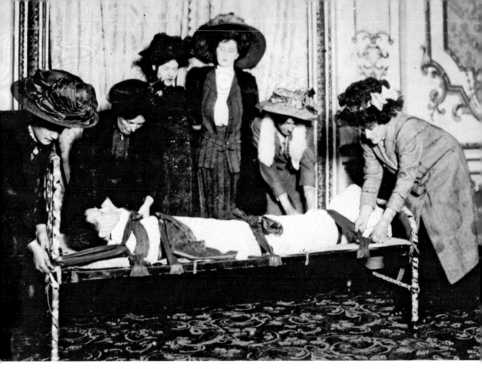

Six women tie Houdini down to a bed built to confine patients. He struggled to free himself in front of audiences—and was greeted with wild applause, night after night.

What was Houdini's secret? Years later, a mechanic who helped with the trick revealed Houdini's method. When Houdini crawled inside the boiler, he hid the pieces of a tiny saw inside his clothes. He quickly removed his handcuffs, assembled the pipe cutter, and sawed

An hour after the committee had riveted him into the tank, Houdini finally opened the curtains and stumbled out, his suit torn and dirty.

through the bolts the committee had riveted in place. He then planned to simply push the top off and replace the real bolts with fake bolts that could be screwed into place.

But once Harry cut the bolts off and pushed, nothing happened. He suddenly realized that when he sawed the bolts, steel edges were left on the sawed-off ends, making them too wide to pass through the holes. Houdini was getting nervous as time passed and the tank got hotter. Then he had an idea. He took apart his pipe cutter to use the narrow end like a spike and the wider end like a hammer. He tapped out the bolts through the holes in the tank. The band, which had been playing their music over and over, concealed the sound of the bolts dropping to the stage floor. He was free! He then quickly replaced the original bolts with his fake rivets and stepped through the curtain to thunderous applause.

The Straitjacket Escape

Houdini continued to do other escapes, including one he had mastered long before but had rarely performed in public. Although Harry had escaped from a straitjacket a few times, he had never had much luck making the escape part of his act. When he slipped behind his onstage cabinet to free himself, the audience simply thought that someone had unbuckled it for him behind the draperies.

But his brother Hardeen stumbled on the solution while performing in Wales. One evening, audience members accused him of having help behind the curtain. Although he was too exhausted from the escape to repeat it and prove he had done it himself, he announced that he would do the straitjacket escape in front of an audience two nights later.

The theater was packed that evening. After he was strapped into the straitjacket, the audience watched him, amazed, as he thrashed about to free his arms and then, once they were free, as he picked at the buckles through the canvas mittens still covering

Houdini's Brother: Escape-Artist Hardeen

Two years younger than Houdini, Theo Weiss shared a love of magic and escapes with his older, more famous brother. In 1901, Houdini renamed his brother "Hardeen" because it sounded like Houdini and would allow Theo to capitalize on Harry's fame. Houdini sent Hardeen on tour in Europe as an escape artist and magician.

Hardeen continued Houdini's act after his brother's death, performing his most famous escapes and magic tricks. This poster advertises the fact that Houdini left his secrets to his brother.

The two brothers liked competing with each other, but Hardeen knew better than to outshine his older brother. Hardeen toured through Europe and America for years, always in his brother's shadow.

Harry and Theo's made-up "fights," created for publicity, hid a deep affection between them.

When Houdini died, he left his equipment and escape secrets to his brother, who continued to tour the world in "The Houdini Show." Two of Houdini's assistants even went to work for Hardeen after Houdini's death. Hardeen died in 1945.

his hands. He had never had such an enthusiastic audience response. He immediately sent his newspaper clippings to Harry.

Harry knew a good thing when he saw it and soon added a straitjacket escape to his act. It turned out to be a great new addition. For the first time, Harry had emerged from behind the curtain to perform an escape, and audiences could see the sheer strength, flexibility, and determination required to succeed at this difficult task. They cheered wildly each time Harry performed it.

Harry and Hardeen often shared tips and tricks. Hardeen was a good magician and escape artist, but he lacked his brother's style and daring. And Harry always wanted the spotlight. Before long, Harry "forgot" that Hardeen had been the first to perform the escape in front of an audience.

A New Water Escape

By late 1907, two years into the American tour, interesting box challenges had become few and far between. Fortunately, by that time Harry and his assistants, Franz Kukol and James Vickery, who had joined them during the tour, were hard at work designing, building, and testing a whole new routine.

Once Harry had taken one last big breath and had sunk beneath the water, the can was topped off with more water and the lid was padlocked shut.

Harry realized he would have to outdo himself. He had an idea for a new escape that he thought would wow the crowd, but he had to get ready. He trained to build up his strength and stamina. He also practiced holding his breath underwater in a huge bathtub he had installed in his home. Bess would time him with a stopwatch, and although he could stay underwater for two-and-a-half minutes, that was not long enough. What he had in mind would require more planning and stamina.

Harry was finally feeling confident that the new escape was ready for an audience. But before he would perform it on stage, it had to pass one last test: Bess. His diary entry for the day he performed it for her says: "Bess . . . saw me do the can trick, thinks it is great. I offered her ten dollars if she could tell me how it was done. She failed to fathom trick. GOOD."

In the new routine, Harry would escape from an iron can that looked like the kind used in dairies to store milk. The can was three and a half feet tall. The sides extended straight up for thirty inches, and then sloped to a neck. It was large enough for Houdini to crouch down inside. But before he was handcuffed and he climbed in, the can was filled with twenty-two large pails of water. Once Harry had taken one last big breath and had sunk beneath the water, the can was topped off with more water and the lid was padlocked shut.

As the band played "Asleep in the Deep," the curtain cabinet was quickly put in place to hide the can. After a

Houdini peeks out from the milk can he introduced to audiences in St. Louis, Missouri, in January 1908. The milk can escape drove audiences back into the theaters again.

minute or so, Franz Kukol would come out from backstage holding an ax over his shoulder, ready to split open the can in case Houdini failed. After about two minutes, Houdini would step out from behind the curtain, soaking wet. Night after night, the audience rose to their feet, cheering.

The secret to the trick was the clever design of the can. The two handles riveted to the sides of the can for carrying it were actually screws holding together two different pieces of the can—inner and outer portions. Once inside the tank, Harry would unscrew the handles. When he stood up, the top and outer cover of the can would rise with him, leaving the rest of the can and the inner casing to hold all the water inside. He would climb out, put the top and outer covering back on, reinsert the screws, and then step out from behind the curtain.

Harry and his assistants had figured out how to bring an underwater escape into the theater. As soon as word of the new routine hit the newspapers, audiences were again clamoring for tickets in each new city on the tour. Handcuff escapes were finally a thing of the past for the Handcuff King.

CHAPTER 6

A Master of Publicity

The easiest way to attract a crowd is to let it be known that at a given time and a given place some one is going to attempt something that in the event of failure will mean sudden death.

From Harry's earliest days performing, he knew the value of publicity. Even when he and Bess barely had enough money to survive, he spent some of it on posters and flyers. They would hand them out on the street to bring audiences into the dime museums and beer halls where they performed. And, like many ads of the time, those would sometimes stretch the truth. A card promoting their Metamorphosis exchange act in 1895 said, "Our act is the supreme cabinet mystery in the World . . . [and] has created a sensation in Europe, Australia, and America," even though it was long before they had ever left the United States.

Houdini also learned that publicity stunts could make a big difference in attracting attention. His escapes from police handcuffs during his early "King of Handcuffs" days brought paying customers into the theaters where he performed across the nation. As Houdini's stunts became more and more dangerous, he knew how to capitalize on them and said, "The easiest way to attract a crowd is to let it be known that at a given time and a given place some one is going to attempt something that in the event of failure will mean sudden death."

A poster promoting Houdini's milk can escape promotes its "death-defying mystery." Houdini loved to emphasize the danger in his act, but every trick was carefully calculated to avoid serious injury.

Publicity Jail Breaks

As his act became bigger, his efforts at promoting it became bigger, too. During the American tour from 1905 to 1908, when his old handcuff escapes were replaced by open escape challenges and the milk can routine, his publicity stunts also became more daring. Now he was staging jailbreaks to attract attention. In Boston in March 1906, he had himself stripped naked, handcuffed, and locked in a cell in the city jail. His clothes were locked in another cell, and the jail's three exits were guarded. He broke out, got his clothes from the other cell, slipped past the guards, ran across the prison yard, and jumped over a prison wall. There he hopped into a waiting car and drove to the Keith Theater where he was performing. He called the police from his dressing room just twenty-three minutes after he had been locked inside the cell.

The stunt that really captured the nation's imagination took place earlier that year in Washington, D.C. While Harry was in town to perform, U.S. officials invited him to the federal jail to "test its locks and inspect the arrangements in Murderers' Row," which then held nine prisoners. Harry was locked in a special cell equipped with a bulletproof oak door that had been built for the notorious Charles J. Guiteau. Guiteau had assassinated

President James Garfield twenty-five years earlier, in 1881, and was held behind this bulletproof door to prevent him from being murdered by revengeful citizens before he could be tried and convicted for his crime.

Walter Hamilton, a man convicted of murdering his wife, was housed in the cell. Harry was stripped of his clothes and put into the cell with Hamilton. In only two minutes Harry had escaped. Rather than simply opening the cell that held his clothes and heading out, though, Harry decided to have some fun. He opened the other cells, moved the nine prisoners around into one another's cells, and locked them up.

"As I was stripped," he recalled later, "the prisoners thought the devil, or someone akin to him, was in their presence, and trembling with fear, they obeyed my command." Then Harry dressed and walked to the warden's office less than half an hour after he was locked away.

"I let all your prisoners out," he said as he entered the office. As the guards jumped up to run to the cell block he quickly added, "But I locked them all in again." The prison staff was speechless. Their cells had clearly failed Houdini's test.

Handcuffs and leg irons lock Houdini inside a Boston prison cell in 1906. Jailbreaks promoting his shows got bigger and bolder in the early 1900s.

The prison staff was speechless. Their cells had clearly failed Houdini's test.

Go Jump off a Bridge

When the weather was good, Houdini switched from jailbreaks to bridge jumps to attract audiences. His underwater training for the milk can trick also came in handy for these daring stunts. Bess would not only time Harry as he held his breath underwater in the enormous tub in their home, but would add bucketfuls of ice to his morning bathwater to help him get used to the low temperatures he'd find deep in the rivers. One time she chilled the water to just above freezing. He even came to like it. "It is getting to be a habit. [I] only feel good after one of those baths," he wrote in his diary.

His first bridge jump of the tour was on Tuesday, November 27, 1906, in Detroit, when he leapt from the Belle Island Bridge into the Detroit River 25 feet below. Earlier that morning, he and Franz Kukol had visited the police storage barn, where they borrowed a coil of heavy rope 113 feet long. Harry also scribbled a will on the back of an envelope in case he did not survive. "I give it all to Bess," was what it said. Several policemen signed it as witnesses and Kukol slipped it into his pocket.

At one that afternoon, stripped of all but his slacks and shivering in the wintry wind, Harry was tied to the rope, which was anchored to the bridge. Then policemen handcuffed him with two of their best sets. Franz Kukol waited below in a small lifeboat. As hundreds of curious people on their lunch breaks watched from the bridge and along the shore, Harry leapt into the water, removed the handcuffs, and popped back to the surface, holding the open cuffs above his head. Then he swam to the waiting boat and climbed inside. His matinee performance that day was sold out.

Harry repeated this routine in big cities around the country

His arms secured with chains and handcuffs, Houdini prepares to leap into the Charles River from Boston's Harvard Bridge in 1908. Such underwater escapes increased his reputation and mystique.

the following spring and summer. He jumped from bridges in Rochester, Pittsburgh (witnessed by an estimated forty thousand), and San Francisco. In San Francisco he added a new and dangerous element. In addition to the handcuffs tying his hands behind his back, Harry had a seventy-five-pound ball chained to one ankle. The weight could have broken his ankle, and certainly would have dragged him to the bottom of the San Francisco Bay if he had been unable to open the cuffs and chain. He did escape, but there are no records of him leaping with a weight on his foot again.

He jumped from bridges in Rochester, Pittsburgh (witnessed by an estimated forty thousand), and San Francisco.

Despite its dangers, Harry continued his bridge jumps. They were a very popular part of his routine. In April 1908, he appeared in Boston, a city that particularly loved him. On May 1, he prepared to jump from the Harvard Bridge into the Charles River. Bess arrived late and tried to get a spot on the nearby pier to watch. A policeman stopped her at the crowded entrance.

"But I'm his wife," she told him.

"Lady," he replied, "that gag don't go. You're the ninth wife of his that has tried to pass here in ten minutes. It'll take you a marriage certificate to get through these lines."

Attracting Attention

One of Houdini's most famous tricks was his escape from a straitjacket while suspended upside down. Before his demonstration, a committee of volunteers would buckle him into the straitjacket, tightening the straps with all their might. Then Houdini would lay down on a platform as his assistant wrapped padding around his ankles and tied them together with heavy rope. Too tight and the rope could break Houdini's ankles. Too loose and he could fall to his death while dangling above the crowd. He would then be hoisted upward by ropes,

Houdini jokes with his assistants as they buckle him into a straitjacket before he attempts an escape from on top of a railroad car in Cleveland, Ohio, in 1915.

feet first, and suspended from the roof of a tall building.

Once in place, Houdini would begin his dramatic struggle, twisting, turning, bending at the waist into a human "L." Once his arms were free, he pulled them back around to unfasten the buckles holding the jacket in place. Houdini performed this astounding feat in every major city in which he appeared for several years in the 1920s. For Houdini, though, it was merely a publicity stunt to attract audiences to his performances in theaters. He saved his *real* tricks for the paying crowds.

Harry Houdini's straitjacket escape was seen by more people than any of his other tricks. How did he do it? In his 1910 book *Handcuff Escapes*, Houdini described his method:

"The first step necessary to free yourself is to place the elbow, which has the continuous hand <u>under</u> the opposite elbow, on some solid foundation and by sheer strength exert sufficient force at this elbow so as to force it gradually up towards the head, and by further persistent straining you can eventually force the head under the lower arm, which results in bringing both of the encased arms in front of the body.

Houdini frees himself from a straitjacket while hanging from a hook above a subway track. Crowds below watch in wonder.

"Once having freed your arms to such an extent as to get them in front of your body, you can now undo the buckles of the straps of the cuffs with your teeth, after which you open the buckles at the back with your hands, which are still encased in the canvas sleeves, and then you remove the straitjacket from your body."

Making an Impression in Print

Harry used his time at home between engagements and during the summer to read the many books he had collected while in Europe and to begin writing a few of his own. In May 1906, he ended the touring season and took the summer off at home. But Harry never rested for long. In September, he published the first issue of *Conjurers' Monthly Magazine*. The magazine included many articles about the history of magic, largely drawn from Harry's considerable collection of books and memorabilia. Producing it was a family affair. Since Harry was performing so much, his brothers Nat, Bill, and Leo all helped with the writing and editing. His brother Hardeen, still touring in Europe, contributed a column about the magic scene there. Harry used the magazine to praise the magicians—past and present—he admired and to skewer those who had slighted or disappointed him.

In the pages of *Conjurers' Monthly* Houdini first wrote about Jean-Eugene Robert-Houdin, the great magician whose memoir had inspired him as a young man and from whom he took his name. During his tour of Europe, he had met with many old

The cover of the second issue of Houdini's *Conjurers' Monthly Magazine*. It was published for only two years before Houdini's attention drifted to other interests.

Houdini's Books

Houdini is shown working at his desk at home in 1925. He collected and studied books on the history of magic and the occult throughout his life.

In 1906, Houdini published his first book, a 96-page booklet called *The Right Way to Do Wrong*. In it, he described the techniques used by counterfeiters, swindlers, con men, mediums, and pickpockets to trick people. He hoped that it would help people to avoid becoming their victims. He sold it in theater lobbies. It was the first of a long list of books, pamphlets, and magazine articles that he would write in the course of his lifetime.

While he traveled through Europe he would write columns about the magic scene there for American magic journals, using a **nom de plume.** He loved to take digs at magicians who had offended him and to support those—like his brother Hardeen—who were his friends.

He was a passionate collector of books about the history of magic and wanted to write a book that would include "biographies, incidents, etc., of every magician, from the time of Moses to the present year." Although he never wrote that, his collection of books on magic was one of the best in the world and was donated to the Library of Congress after he died.

magicians. He wanted to learn everything he could from them about the history of magic. Several of them suggested that others had originated the tricks that Robert-Houdin had made popular. He was disappointed to learn that his hero may not have been the innovator he had thought.

Houdini took his quest for the truth to the extreme. In *Conjurers' Monthly*, and later in a book titled *The Unmasking of Robert-Houdin*, he attacked his former idol and left his reputation in tatters. Many magicians said Houdini had been unfair and that he had many facts wrong. He was not a careful researcher, and he let his passions take control of his pen. Anyone who betrayed him, living or dead, would feel his wrath.

Many magicians said Houdini had been unfair and that he had many facts wrong. Anyone who betrayed him, living or dead, would feel his wrath.

In 1908, after two years, the magazine was closed down. Harry had too many other activities going on to continue it, and he had begun to lose interest in magazine publishing as he and Bess were setting off to Germany on tour. Harry's mother saw them off at the pier in New York. After the ship sailed out of sight, she returned to the big house on West 113th Street, where she wound up the family's grandfather clock. It would continue to tick as long as Harry was away, so that it could measure the time until he returned to her again.

CHAPTER 7

A New Passion—Flying

Never in any fear and never in any danger.
It is a wonderful thing.

While appearing in Hamburg, Germany, in the fall of 1909, Harry Houdini fell in love. Bess had nothing to fear, though. The object of his affection was an airplane. He had seen German aviator Hans Grade demonstrate a French **biplane**, called a Voisin, over a nearby racetrack. Within a week, he owned the same kind of plane and had hired French mechanic Antonio Brassac to care for it and teach him to fly.

Orville Wright takes control in the first airplane flight in history as his brother Wilbur stands on the ground. He flew at Kitty Hawk, North Carolina, on December 17, 1903.

Since Wilbur and Orville Wright successfully flew the first airplane at Kitty Hawk, North Carolina, in 1903, the sky had become the new frontier for adventurers. By 1909, flight records were being made and broken throughout the U.S. and Europe. Harry was in England that summer when Louis Bleriot first flew across the English Channel, an achievement that made news around the world.

Harry had been attracted to planes since the earliest days of flight and had wanted to incorporate them into a routine. In 1908, he told reporters that he had offered $5,000 to use a Wright Brothers plane for a daring escape in London. His plan was to fly over London's West End, handcuffed, and parachute, while escaping from the cuffs, into the city's popular Piccadilly Circus area. Technical difficulties had prevented this daring feat, but his fascination continued.

Like the Wright Brothers' first plane, the Voisin had two sets of wings, but these were each made of two boxes or "cells," and the tail was shaped like another box. Bicycle wheels supported the wings and tail, and the nose had a single wheel to allow it to roll in case the plane landed headfirst. It was powered by an eight-cylinder, sixty-horsepower engine and weighed about 1,300 pounds.

Learning to Fly

During Houdini's two-month run at the Hansa Theater in Hamburg, he did double duty. Each morning, he would travel to a parade ground where the German Army allowed him to store his plane. Their only request was that Houdini show the German officers the basics of flight. Houdini's mechanic, Antonio Brassac, spent several weeks putting the plane together and getting the engine tuned. Houdini posed proudly beside his new toy even before he had taken his first flight. While Brassac tinkered with the plane, Houdini practiced the simple movements of the controls that would raise, lower, and turn the plane when he could finally reach the sky.

Brassac started the engine and Houdini took off on his very first flight.

Once Brassac got the engine working, the weather was too windy to fly the flimsy plane. Finally, the skies cleared. Brassac started the engine and Houdini took off on his very first flight. He rose only a few feet before the plane crashed to the ground, nose first, breaking the propeller. Houdini was not hurt, but he had to spend another two weeks waiting for replacement parts.

Harry Houdini made his first successful flight on November 26, 1909. It lasted less than two minutes, but the fifty people gathered on the field to witness it were thrilled as they looked in the sky at the plane with Houdini sitting inside and HOUDINI painted outside. He continued practicing his flying skills as he traveled from Germany to France.

Earlier that year, Harry Rickards, an Australian vaudeville theater owner, saw Houdini's show in England. Rickards offered the escape artist the highest salary he had ever paid an act to perform in that southern continent. Not only that, but he said he would pay Harry his salary for the twelve weeks that he would be sailing and relaxing there as well as for the twelve weeks he would be performing. Houdini was ecstatic. His contracts in Europe would delay his performance in Australia, but he immediately began making plans for his tour, which would begin in February 1910.

Houdini had learned that no one had flown in Australia before, and he was determined to be the first. At the end of 1909, Brassac took apart the plane and packed the pieces in large crates

The Birth of Flight

Harry Houdini's first flight in 1909 was only six years after Wilbur and Orville Wright designed and successfully flew the first airplane.

French aviation pioneers Charles and Gabriel Voisin are pictured in this undated photograph. In 1909 Houdini bought one of their biplanes and learned how to to fly.

On December 17, 1903, Orville Wright became the first to fly after the brothers tossed a coin. Wilbur had his turn on the next flight, later the same day. The Wrights' plane was a biplane, which meant that it had two sets of wings. The pilot lay on the lower set of wings and moved his hips to help control the direction of the flight. The Wright Flyer, as the plane was called, is now on display at the National Air and Space Museum in Washington, D.C.

The world soon had flying fever, and new planes were being developed in Europe and America. The Voisin biplane flown by Houdini was designed by two other flying brothers, Gabriel and Charles Voisin. Their 1907 model, which Houdini flew, became a favorite among European flyers. The Voisins built more than seventy-five of them between 1907 and 1912.

With the beginning of World War I in 1914, airplanes were transformed from a gentleman's toy to a military weapon. Planes were quickly used to spy on enemy troops, drop bombs, and carry information. That year, a French pilot in a Voisin plane is credited with the first air combat victory, when he used a machine gun to down a German fighter plane.

Harry Houdini flies above a crowd in his Voisin biplane in 1910. He loved giving demonstrations to curious crowds, many of whom had never seen a plane in flight before.

for the long journey. He also crated up many spare parts for the plane that they bought during a visit to the Voisin factory in Paris. They loaded all the crates on the *Malwa*, the ship that would take them to Australia, and pulled from the dock in Marseilles in early January.

Flying Down Under

After the month-long journey to Australia, Harry, Bess, and Brassac traveled to Melbourne, where Harry was booked to perform. Harry rented space at a field at Digger's Rest, about twenty miles from the city, and bought a large tent to protect the plane. Brassac worked all day uncrating and rebuilding the plane. Harry rushed out there before dawn every morning and performed back in Melbourne each afternoon and evening.

In the same field sat a Wright plane owned by Ralph Banks, who ran an automobile garage in Melbourne. Like Harry, Banks was hoping to be the first man to fly in Australia. On March 1, 1910, Ralph Banks decided to take his chance, even though the winds were dangerously strong. He rose about twelve feet before the plane crashed and broke into pieces on the ground. Banks had a black eye and cuts on his face but was otherwise all right. Harry rushed to the crash site and helped pick up the pieces of the shattered plane. Banks was no longer Harry's rival to be the first man to fly successfully in Australia, and the two became friends.

On the morning of March 18, 1910, Houdini made three short flights, including one that lasted longer than three minutes and carried him about a hundred feet over the field.

By the middle of the month, Houdini's Voisin was ready to fly. Now the weather had to cooperate. Each morning, a small crowd would come out to the field hoping to witness the continent's first successful flight. On the morning of March 18, 1910, Houdini made three short flights, including one that lasted longer than three minutes and carried him about a hundred feet over the field. The crowd below was delirious, and no one was more excited than Antonio Brassac, who had lovingly assembled the plane each day and slept beside it each night. Official witnesses to the flight included Ralph Banks, Harry's former competitor for the honor.

"Never in any fear and never in any danger. It is a wonderful thing," Harry Houdini wrote in his diary that night.

Two days later he repeated his feat for a photographer. The winds were gusty, and the little plane was "blown about like a piece of paper on a windy day," Houdini wrote in his diary. But he "made a landing safe and sound."

News of the flight made the front pages of Australia's major newspapers. But word soon spread that a young man near Sydney, Fred Custance, had flown a day earlier in a Bleriot monoplane. He rose only about twelve feet above the ground. And on his second flight, as he tried to climb, he lost control and crashed. Custance's

Houdini's Voisin biplane is returned to its tent after his successful flight in Digger's Rest, Australia.

attempt did not follow the rules for official recorded flight by the Federation Aeronautique International, the group that was set up to regulate flight a year earlier. Nonetheless, Harry was distressed that his record was in question.

In the days following, Houdini flew in front of larger crowds who were excited to witness the achievement. He was determined to set new records for time in the air and distance traveled. One

This trophy was awarded to Houdini by the Aerial League of Australia for being the first man to fly in Australia. The trophy mistakenly says March 16, 1910, but he actually flew on March 18.

day the following week he stayed in the air for seven minutes, thirty-seven seconds, landing perfectly afterward. As one reporter put it, his accomplishments over the week following his first flight "fully established his claim to be considered the first successful aviator in Australia."

> As one reporter put it, his accomplishments over the week following his first flight "fully established his claim to be considered the first successful aviator in Australia."

When Harry finished his performances in Melbourne, Harry, Bess, and Brassac traveled across the country to Sydney, where he began a six-week run in late March. Harry tried to fly at Rosehill racetrack in Sydney before hundreds of people. After several rocky starts, weather delays, and short hops in the air, on May 1, Houdini made what he called "the flight of my life."

Shortly after he took off, about twenty feet above ground, the plane suddenly dipped, and those watching were certain he would crash. But at the last moment, Houdini pulled the controls upward, and the Voisin rose to one hundred fifty feet and circled over the racetrack. A sudden crosscurrent smacked it sideways, but he managed to turn into the wind and straighten out the plane. Another gust sent it rushing toward the ground again, and spectators said it came within three feet of the tents assembled on the field. Houdini pulled up quickly again and circled the field once more before landing. As he touched ground smoothly, he turned off the engine to taxi to a stop. But he suddenly realized he was speeding toward one of the horses' hurdles that had not been cleared from the field. He pulled up on the controls and lifted the plane at the last minute to sail over the hurdle and then

Harry Houdini behind the controls of his biplane in Australia. After he became the first to fly in Australia, he had his plane dismantled and never flew it again.

landed again. Antonio Brassac called it the most sensational flight he had ever seen. Men and women cheered.

Despite Houdini's claim in Sydney that after he was forgotten as the Handcuff King he would be remembered in Australia as "the first man to fly there in a machine heavier than air," he was already losing his enthusiasm for flying. He loved to win. Once he had won, though, his attention would move on to the next challenge.

Houdini probably piloted an airplane twenty times in Europe and Australia, spending little more than an hour in the air altogether. Soon Brassac was taking the plane apart again as they prepared to leave for home. The plane would never be reassembled for Houdini again.

CHAPTER 8

In Search of the Next Big Trick

To say the applause was deafening is putting it too mildly.

—Review from a London newspaper

After Harry's triumph in the skies above Australia, he and Bess headed home for a summer's rest. In August 1910, they returned to England to tour. When they arrived, Houdini discovered that while he had been gone, a number of Houdini imitators had appeared on the scene. One of them, a woman who performed under the name of Empress, had developed a near duplicate of his act, including a straitjacket escape and the water can trick.

Despite the enthusiasm of audiences throughout Europe, Harry knew he would need a new trick that would be so difficult that no one would follow in his footsteps anytime soon. From the moment his ship had pulled out of New York, he began sketching ideas for the "next big thing."

In England he hired a new assistant named Jim Collins, an expert carpenter and metalworker who was clever and careful and could take Houdini's wildest ideas and turn them into reality. By early 1911, they had developed the perfect trick: one that was so challenging to perform that few would try to copy it, and so amazing to witness that audiences would flock to theaters again. They called it the "Chinese Water Torture Cell." Once they had

The Chinese Water Torture Cell was Houdini's most amazing escape trick. Although he perfected it in 1911 in London, he waited until 1912 to introduce it to his act.

perfected it, Harry dismantled it and stored it in a warehouse he had rented in London. He would save it until he needed a big career boost.

Strange Escapes

Houdini's European tour was a huge success, with audiences challenging him to escape from everything from a sea bag, which was used to restrain drunken sailors, to the barrel of a lighted steel cannon. When he returned home that fall, he found that his American fans were never at a loss for strange escape challenges, either.

One of the weirdest occurred in Boston. A "sea monster," which looked like a cross between an octopus and a whale (and may have been an elephant seal), had been caught off the coast. The sea monster had been cleaned out and preserved by a local taxidermist. The lieutenant governor of Massachusetts and some local businessmen challenged Harry to escape from inside it. Harry gladly accepted. A dozen men hauled the huge creature on to the stage of the Keith's Theatre. Houdini slipped inside through a slit and had his hands and feet cuffed. The committee closed the slit with chains and wrapped more chains around the huge carcass. Harry brought along perfume to spray near his face to cover the ghastly odors. Fifteen minutes after the curtains were placed around the beast, Harry emerged, greasy and a bit woozy from the chemicals used to preserve his marine prison.

Sometimes the challenges were pretty standard, but the challengers took things too far. When some committee members tightened the straps of a challenge bag in Detroit, they pulled them so tight that one of the buckles pushed into Houdini's back so hard

When he returned home that fall, he found that his American fans were never at a loss for strange escape challenges, either.

that it burst a blood vessel in his kidney. He was sick for two weeks, dragging himself through his performances, before he finally saw a doctor in Pittsburgh. The doctor ordered him to bed immediately and warned him that if he did not stop straining his body he would be "dead within a year."

"You don't know me," Harry replied.

But even Houdini knew he could not simply keep working through his current condition. He finished his last performances in Pittsburgh and cancelled his engagements for two weeks to go home and rest. Then he headed back to work—escaping from a packing case, a mail pouch, even a cask filled with beer. Soon he realized he had gone back on the road too soon. He was thirty eight years old and the wear and tear on his body was beginning to show. His damaged kidney continued to trouble him throughout his life.

Although his body felt the effects of decades of tough treatment, he kept going, and each year, Harry would send his doctor a photo of himself performing his latest escape with a note saying, "Still alive and going strong."

The Underwater Box Escape

Although Harry Houdini had played to good crowds in New York, he had never received the kind of enthusiastic attention in newspapers that greeted him throughout the rest of the world. He was determined to break through in the New York press, and in July 1912 he did just that. He announced that he would escape from handcuffs inside a packing box dropped into the East River. Even the big city editors had to pay attention to that. The New York City police had warned him that he would not be permitted to jump into the river, so on the morning of the escape, Harry arranged for the box to be placed on a barge pulled by a tugboat far enough from shore to be

Secured in handcuffs, chains, and leg irons, and locked in a packing box, Houdini is lowered into the water for one of his breathtaking escapes. He repeated this daring trick in major cities throughout the country.

outside police jurisdiction. Along with the box came a complement of reporters. Three ferryboats filled with passengers gathered nearby to watch.

After Harry's hands and feet were bound, he climbed inside a box twenty-four inches wide, thirty-six inches high, and thirty-four inches long. Harry got the reporters to help hammer the nails in place to seal the box shut, and to help secure it with ropes and steel bands. They tied two hundred pounds of iron to the sides of the box to make certain that it would sink. Then the crew shoved the box down a ramp and overboard. The box floated, only its top visible, in the water nearby. Less than a minute later, Harry's head popped above the surface and he swam to a nearby rowboat. The passengers on the ferries cheered.

Less than a minute later, Harry's head popped above the surface and he swam to a nearby rowboat. The passengers on the ferries cheered.

The box was dragged back onto the barge. The reporters were mystified. The box was still held together by the ropes and bands. When they opened it, they found the handcuffs and leg irons inside. Even the *New York Times* covered the story, and *Scientific American*, not a magazine to cover escape artists, called it "one of the most remarkable tricks ever performed."

For Houdini, though, his greatest thrill occurred at the end of his first week at Hammerstein's Roof Garden. He asked to be paid his salary—$1,000—in gold coins. He took the heavy bag of coins to his dressing room, where one of his assistants, Jim Vickery, was waiting with polish. The two men buffed up each coin until it shone. Then Harry rushed home and ran into the room where his mother was sitting.

Houdini's Injuries

Harry Houdini poses for a portrait around 1910. He was beginning to feel the effects of his physically challenging performances, but he rarely rested. He hated to disappoint his audiences.

Early in 1912, Houdini pulled a ligament in his back during an escape, and he suffered from occasional broken bones and strains. But Houdini considered them all part of the job. During one underwater escape, he was knocked unconscious when he dove into a pool, handcuffed, and hit his head on the bottom. His assistants had to drag him from the pool before he drowned. And once, as twenty thousand people watched, he dove from the pier in Atlantic City, New Jersey, and crashed into a sandbar, nearly breaking his neck.

Once on tour in England, a local body builder took Houdini up on his standard challenge that he would give twenty-five British pounds to anyone who could put him in handcuffs from which he could not escape. The man wrapped him so tightly in chains, padlocks, and six pairs of handcuffs that Houdini's arms and hands were blue from lack of blood flowing to them. When he stumbled out from behind the curtain, his arms and legs looked, "as though a tiger had clawed him," said one witness.

"Mama, do you remember the promise I made Father years ago that I would always look after you?"

"Of course, I remember," she said.

"Hold out your apron."

Then he poured the glittering coins onto her lap. Later he said that moment was the greatest thrill of his life.

The Chinese Water Torture Cell

Houdini's popularity had never been greater. He decided it was time to mystify his audiences once again with an act that even he could not top. On September 21, 1912, while on tour in Germany, Harry finally performed in public the trick that he had developed more than a year earlier. It was to become his most amazing trick and one that, even today, holds its secrets. The Chinese Water Torture Cell, or the Upside Down as Harry referred to it in his notes, was a box about the size of a phone booth. The frame was made of mahogany and steel, and the sides were of tempered half-inch glass held in place with watertight seals. The removable top was a stock, which opened like a jaw and was fitted with two holes through which his ankles were secured.

He took several deep breaths, then signaled for them to lower him into the cell, headfirst.

Harry appeared onstage in a swimming suit at the Circus Busch in Berlin and lay down on a mat near the chamber. After his assistant, Jim Collins, secured his ankles in the stock, a box-like steel frame was placed around him to reduce the chance of him being hurt when he was raised above the box. While he was being secured, his other assistants were busy filling the cell with warm water. Then ropes were attached to the frame and stock, which slowly pulled Houdini up, feet first, and positioned him, upside down, above the cell.

He took several deep breaths, then signaled for them to lower him into the cell, headfirst. After a steel lid was put over the top of the cell and padlocked, the cell was quickly surrounded by drapes. Within only two minutes, Houdini, soaking wet and breathless, was pulling back the curtains. Behind him stood the cell, still locked and full of water.

The audience stood and roared for many minutes as Harry bowed and smiled from the stage. "To say the applause was deafening is putting it too mildly," said one reviewer. The trick was so mind-boggling that some were convinced he used supernatural powers to achieve it.

In the summer of 1913, Hammerstein's Roof Garden in New York engaged Harry for another two-week run in the middle of his European tour. He accepted, knowing he would see his mother again. She seemed weaker each time he visited her, and he hated to be away for too long. That summer, he performed the Upside Down for the first time in America at Hammerstein's, and his mother sat proudly in the audience, beaming at her son's triumph.

A Sad Farewell

When Harry Houdini set sail for Copenhagen, Denmark, in July 1913 to continue his European tour, he did not know that he was seeing his mother for the last time. Cecelia Weiss seemed to know, though, that her end was near.

"Ehrich, perhaps I won't be here when you return," she said to him on the pier where she had stood so many times to see him off on his tours. He tried to make her laugh by reminding her that she had been saying that same thing for years.

After one more hug and kiss, she told him to "get along in God's name." He was the last person to board the ship. She

Houdini's Off-Stage Inventions

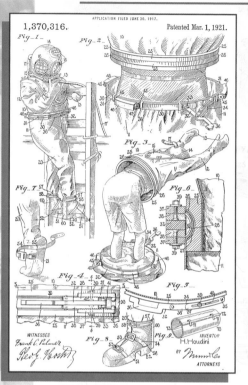

1,370,316.
APPLICATION FILED JUNE 30, 1917.
Patented Mar. 1, 1921.

Fig_1.
Fig_2.
Fig_3.
Fig_6.
Fig_7.
Fig_4.
Fig_5.
Fig_8.
Fig_9.

WITNESSES
Frank C. Palmer
Geof. Mosks

INVENTOR
H. Houdini
BY
ATTORNEYS

Houdini's invention of a two-piece diving suit was granted a patent in 1921. The patent illustration shows the amount of detail that Houdini gave to his invention.

Houdini and his assistants did not limit their creativity just to the stage. Houdini invented a diving suit he hoped would save lives during emergencies. Earlier diving suits developed in the 1700s were one piece and made of leather. Houdini's two-piece suit, divided at the waist, let divers put it on themselves and—more important—allowed them to take it off within seconds underwater so they could swim to the surface in case of an emergency. Although the suit does not seem to have been used by divers, Houdini did receive patents in the U.S. and Great Britain.

Not all of Houdini's inventions were so serious. He also patented a wind-up toy that escaped from a straitjacket when put upside down on its head.

smiled and waved and called to him to bring her back a pair of slippers as a souvenir. He threw a streamer to her from the ship and she caught it. They both held on to their ends of the paper

Harry Houdini kisses his mother, Cecelia Weiss, in this 1908 photograph. A devoted son, he called her "an angel on earth in human form." He was devastated when she died in 1913.

until the ship pulled out and the streamer broke, falling into the river.

By the time Harry and Bess reached Hamburg a week later, Cecelia Weiss had suffered a stroke and was paralyzed. In the days before telephones, communication was difficult. Harry and Bess had already taken a midnight train to Copenhagen before a telegram caught up with them telling Harry that his mother was very ill. He was performing that evening before members of the

Harry Houdini visits his mother's grave in 1914. It was the first place he would come when he returned home from his tours. His father was also buried here.

Danish royal family. Right afterward, while at a reception, he received another message saying his mother was dead. When he opened it, Houdini fainted.

He and Bess rushed to the train station that night and reached Hamburg in time to return home on the same ship that had brought them to Europe. He cabled his brother Hardeen and told him to postpone the funeral until he could get there.

When Harry and Bess arrived in New York, he rushed into the parlor of their home, where his mother lay waiting to be buried. His heart was broken. He walked through the next weeks unable to think of anything but his grief. "I who have laughed at the terrors of death, who have smilingly leaped from bridges, received a shock from which I do not think recovery is possible," he wrote. He never did. He missed her terribly for the rest of his life. It was as though a light had gone out inside him, a light that would never shine again.

CHAPTER 9

Houdini in Hollywood

houdinize—to release or extricate oneself from (confinement, bonds, or the like), as by wriggling out.

—Funk & Wagnalls dictionary, 1920 edition

For months after the death of his mother, Harry Houdini seemed like a ghost walking through life. He returned to touring in September 1913, opening in Nuremburg, Germany, but while the audiences were enthusiastic, he felt numb inside. The following spring brought him some excitement, and for a little while he seemed like his old self.

When he booked passage back to New York on the *Imperator* for Bess and himself, the agent whispered to him that none other than former president Theodore Roosevelt was sailing on the same ship. Harry headed straight to the offices of London's *Telegraph*. The newspaper had just begun running a series by Roosevelt—who was a great adventurer—about his recent expedition in South America. One of Harry's reporter friends showed him a map of the trip and some other information from stories that had not yet been published.

During an evening performance for the guests, Harry

Harry headed straight to the offices of London's Telegraph.

Harry Houdini stands with Theodore Roosevelt (center) on the SS *Imperator* in 1814. Houdini's "mind reading" trick there astonished the former president, who wondered if otherworldly powers were involved.

asked them to write down a question on a piece of paper that he would try to answer through magic. By some sleight of hand, Harry managed to see that Roosevelt had written "Where was I last Christmas?" It was exactly the question he had hoped for. Harry used a pair of two-sided blackboards, each about the size of a piece of paper. He showed the

audience that they were blank. (He tricked the audience into thinking they had seen all four sides, but they had really only seen three.) Then he tied the two slates together and asked Roosevelt to drop his folded-up question in between them. When he opened up the slates, the answer to Roosevelt's question was there: a map of the river basin through which Roosevelt had traveled during the holiday.

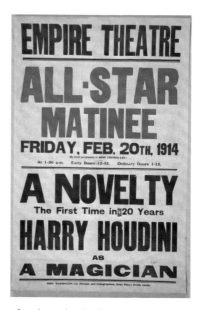

EMPIRE THEATRE
ALL-STAR MATINEE
FRIDAY, FEB. 20TH, 1914

At 1-30 p.m.   Early Doors 12-45.   Ordinary Doors 1-15.

A NOVELTY
The First Time in 20 Years
HARRY HOUDINI
AS
A MAGICIAN

After the outbreak of World War I in Europe in 1914, Houdini introduced more magic tricks into his act. A poster announces Houdini's rare appearance as a magician.

Always looking for the biggest and best, Houdini made Jennie, a 10,000-pound elephant, disappear at the Hippodrome in New York in 1918.

Houdini's War Effort

From 1914 to 1918 much of the Western world was embroiled in conflict. The Great War, as it was then called, pitted the Allied Powers (France, Great Britain, Russia, Italy, Japan, and, from 1917, the United States) against the Central Powers (Germany, Austria-Hungary, and Turkey). During those years, more than eight million soldiers died from wounds or disease, and the face of Europe was changed forever.

During the war years, Houdini was unable to appear in Europe as a performer. He tried to enlist as a soldier in 1917, when the United States entered the war, but the army said he was too old at forty-three to fight. He made his own contributions to the war effort, entertaining thousands of troops at American army bases and planning a huge benefit for families of troops who had been killed. He also visited many army hospitals, doing shows for patients who had been injured in the war.

The former president was astounded. Later he asked Houdini, "man to man," if supernatural forces were at work in the trick. "No, Colonel," Houdini replied. "Just hokus-pokus."

Houdini's "hokus-pokus" continued to amaze audiences over the next few years, as he introduced more magic into his act. He made an elephant disappear, and he walked through a brick wall that he had workmen construct in front of the audience. But times were changing. World War I broke out in Europe later that year, decimating a generation of young men. It would be another five years before Harry would return to the countries in which he first found fame.

Movie Mania

As Harry toured the U.S., dazzling the public with his upside-down straitjacket escapes from the sides of skyscrapers and amazing theater audiences with his Chinese Water Torture Cell, vaudeville itself was being threatened. In 1905, the first motion picture theater opened. Only four years later there were eight thousand movie theaters, bringing song, dance, and drama to audiences at a fraction of the cost of vaudeville live entertainment. While some people in vaudeville saw movies as a passing fad or felt threatened by them, Harry Houdini embraced this new way to entertain audiences.

In 1918, Houdini made his first film, called *The Master Mystery*, for a new company called the Octagon Film Corporation. It was made as a fifteen-episode serial movie. Back then, people would go to movies each week to see the latest installment in a continuing story, just as people today watch the latest weekly episode of their favorite programs on television. In *The Master Mystery*, Houdini plays Quentin Locke, an undercover agent for the Justice Department, who is investigating the evil International Patents Incorporated. The corrupt company pretends to help inventors market their latest inventions, but instead keeps them hidden so that its own companies can continue to grow

This poster promotes an episode in *The Master Mystery*, Houdini's first movie, in 1918. Audiences would return to theaters each week to see the next installment of the film.

Houdini in a movie still from *The Master Mystery*. Each episode ended with Houdini in an impossible situation, and each began with his daring escape from the previous peril.

without having to develop new products.

The action takes place in a huge mansion called Brentwood that includes hidden panels and underground rooms. The movie features an evil mechanical character called "Automaton." It was the first robot to appear in a popular movie.

Every episode ended with Houdini (and often the beautiful daughter of one of the owners of International Patents) in some difficult predicament from which he would escape at the beginning of the next installment. In the course of the movie, he escapes from a straitjacket, naturally, an underwater diving suit, an electric chair, and the bottom of an elevator shaft as the elevator slowly sinks toward him.

He did all his own stunts for the movie and, according to Bess, suffered from three broken bones in his left wrist and seven black eyes. The black eyes healed quickly enough, but the broken wrist troubled him for months afterward.

The Master Mystery played all around the world, bringing Houdini new audiences as far away as Asia, where he had never performed. Unfortunately, Octagon Film Corporation went bankrupt, and Harry had to sue them to receive his share of the profits from the film. For his next two films, he chose a more stable company, Famous Players-Lasky Corporation, which later became Paramount. In 1919, he and Bess headed to California, where they rented a bungalow and settled for a time into what would be the closest they would ever come to stable, nine-to-five lives.

Life in Los Angeles

The Houdinis loved the weather in Los Angeles and had fond memories of performing there. They enjoyed seeing and being seen by movie stars. They met Charlie Chaplin, king of silent comedy, and Gloria Swanson, queen of silent drama, and many others. In 1920, the Funk and Wagnalls dictionary added a new verb entry, which read: "houdinize—to release or extricate oneself from (confinement, bonds, or the like), as by wriggling out."

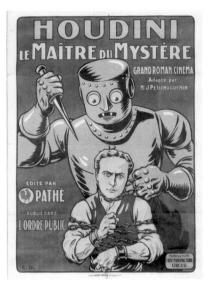

A French poster promotes *The Master Mystery*. The film features an evil creature named Automaton, the first robot in a popular movie. The movie brought Houdini new fans around the world.

The Birth of Motion Pictures

In 1919, Hollywood, a suburb of Los Angeles, was becoming the center of American moviemaking, and the early 1920s saw the birth of every type of movie watched today, from comedies to dramas to romances and even science fiction. One of the earliest stars of Hollywood comedies was Charlie Chaplin, whose movies are still studied by film students and still make people laugh out loud. Another comedy star was Buster Keaton. The Houdinis worked with Keaton's parents in a traveling show very early in their careers. Houdini claimed that he had given the comedy star his nickname of "Buster" when he was a boy.

Adventure movies, like the type that Houdini made, were also very popular. Douglas Fairbanks was one of Hollywood's most popular stars, playing Zorro, Robin Hood, and romantic pirates in many movies. Handsome and athletic, he influenced romantic leading men in adventure films for generations.

Like many early movie stars, comedian Buster Keaton (far right) began in vaudeville as a child with his parents. The family is seen together in this photograph c. 1900. Harry and Bess often performed with them early in their career.

Houdini was now a real celebrity. For Harry, though, the greatest treat of living in Los Angeles was that he could spend time with Harry Kellar, dean of American magicians, and a man Houdini loved and admired. They spent hours swapping stories, and Kellar showed him several secrets he had shared with no other magicians.

While Houdini lived in Hollywood, he enjoyed swapping stories and tricks with his hero, Harry Kellar, one of the greatest American magicians. Kellar is shown in this 1897 poster advertising his act.

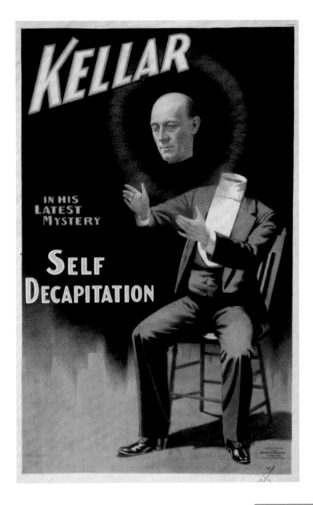

Houdini in a publicity photo for *The Grim Game* in 1919. The film's breathtaking plane crash scene was actually performed by a stunt double after Houdini broke his wrist.

Life in Los Angeles was not one long vacation, though. Houdini soon began shooting his second movie, *The Grim Game*. Like his first film, it was filled with daredevil stunts, including a jailbreak and a straitjacket escape while dangling from a rope hanging from the roof of a building. He broke his wrist again during one of the jail sequences and had his arm in a sling as he watched from the ground as a stunt double performed what was to become the most amazing sequence in the movie.

The script called for Houdini's character to leap from one plane to another while in the air. As the two planes approached, a stiff wind pushed one into the other, and they locked together and began spinning toward the ground. The director and cameraman kept filming from a third plane. Just as the planes neared the ground they separated, then crashed, surprisingly gently, into a nearby bean field. Fortunately, no one was badly hurt. The footage was spectacular, so the director had the scene written into the script. For years Houdini kept quiet about the fact that the great escape artist had watched it all safely from the ground.

Houdini Pictures

In 1919, after *The Grim Game* was finished, Houdini headed back to Europe to fulfill contracts he had been unable to honor during the years of World War I. Before he left, though, he decided he had learned enough about the movie business to produce his own films. He even brought along a camera on tour to shoot street scenes in London, Paris, and Edinburgh.

When he returned home in the summer, he threw himself into moviemaking. His first independent movie under the Houdini Picture Corporation was *The Man from Beyond*. In it he played Howard Hillary, a man who had been frozen for a century inside a wall of ice in the Arctic. Earlier on, Harry had dreamed of escaping from a solid block of ice onstage. So in the movie, he got to perform a variation of his imagined trick. But the movie's big scene involved him rescuing the heroine as her canoe rushed toward Niagara Falls. He was attached to shore by a wire in case something went wrong, but the amazing rescue was carried out by Houdini himself.

Houdini went all out in promoting the movie. It premiered in New York in April 1922 along with a half-hour live magic and escape show, including his disappearing elephant trick. The live show element worked so well that he put together traveling shows, each headed by an accomplished magician, to appear

HOUDINI PICTURE CORPORATION

presents

HOUDINI

in

"THE MAN FROM BEYOND

The poster for *The Man from Beyond*, the first film by the Houdini Picture Corporation. Even live magic shows staged before the movie failed to attract audiences.

with the film around the country. Despite his huge promotional efforts, the movie attracted only medium-sized audiences, and his company lost money on it.

Houdini's final movie was *Haldane of the Secret Service*, which featured Harry fighting counterfeiters. It lacked the kind of heart-pounding effects of his other movies. People only came to Houdini movies for the amazing escapes, and without them there was very little in the movie to attract an audience. Reviewers had hardly a kind word to say about it and theatergoers stayed away.

Houdini closed down Houdini Pictures after the failure of

Haldane. He was quickly losing interest in moviemaking and had found a new obsession. In the years during and following World War I, people had become curious about spiritualism, which suggested it was possible to communicate with the spirits of the dead through people with special powers called mediums. Harry had done his share of medium acts in his dime museum days, and he knew a con when he saw one. He was ready to leave the make-believe world of movies to take on a far more sinister one. In spiritualism, mediums were taking advantage of people who grieved for their lost loved ones. Harry quickly became their most passionate foe.

Houdini in a publicity still for *The Man from Beyond* in 1921. A powerful swimmer, Houdini performed a daring river rescue of his heroine near Niagara Falls.

CHAPTER 10

The Magician and the Mediums

I have never seen or heard anything that could convince one there is a possibility of communication with the loved ones who have gone beyond.

When Harry and Bess Houdini were barely making a living with variety shows and circuses, Harry had watched several mediums as they did séances for people hoping to speak to dead loved ones. He quickly caught on to their tricks. When business was slow with one traveling show, Harry performed a "fully lit séance" as part of the performance. He made spirit hands materialize, caused musical instruments to fly through the air, and gave messages from "beyond" to audience members. He would do careful research in each town they visited, walking through the cemetery to gather names of those who had died recently, and talking with newspaper reporters and local gossips about recent events. In one of these séances in Galena, Kansas, he claimed to be seeing a man named Efram Alexander who had been murdered. Suddenly several men sitting in the very back of the theater panicked, jumped up, and ran out the back door.

Harry quickly became uncomfortable with the medium act. It was one thing to entertain people with his skills, but another to take advantage of their beliefs. "I felt that the game had gone far enough," he later wrote. "I most certainly did not relish the idea of treading on the sacred feelings of my admirers." He vowed to give up the medium business, but his education in its methods served him well when he decided to take it on in the 1920s.

Houdini Meets the Creator of Sherlock Holmes

Spiritualism became very popular during and just after World War I, and some famous authors and scientists became intrigued by the idea of spirits floating in another world. The amazing discoveries of that period, including radio waves, electricity, and Einstein's theory of relativity, made many people think that anything was possible.

The most famous believer in spiritualism was Sir Arthur Conan Doyle, adventurer, medical doctor, and creator of Sherlock Holmes—Doyle's literary detective who relied on powers of observation and reason to solve mysteries. Unlike his

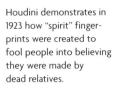

Houdini demonstrates in 1923 how "spirit" finger-prints were created to fool people into believing they were made by dead relatives.

brilliant, always rational creation, Doyle was such a believer in the spirit world that he would cling to his faith in mediums even when they admitted that they were fakes. Houdini and Doyle met when Harry was touring in England after World War I. Sir Arthur and Lady Doyle invited Harry to lunch, where Harry **soft-pedaled** his opinions on mediums out of respect for his host. Doyle was convinced he had spoken several times with the spirit of his son, who had died in World War I. Harry led Doyle to believe that he had an open mind about spiritualism and asked him for introductions to some of the most famous mediums of the day in England. His claim was not too far from the truth. He did hope that people, particularly his mother, could communicate from the next world, but his skills as a magician made believing in the power of any mediums he had seen impossible.

As Harry toured in Europe and throughout America, he arranged to meet with local mediums to learn more about their techniques. With each new experience, he became more convinced that he was the best person to shatter their power over people. In late 1922, Harry published an article in a New York

Harry Houdini shakes hands with Sir Arthur Conan Doyle as Sir Arthur prepares to return to England after an American lecture tour in 1922.

Sir Arthur Conan Doyle

Sir Arthur Conan Doyle, who was a medical doctor, is best known as the creator of Sherlock Holmes. He modeled Holmes after one of his professors of medicine, Dr. Joseph Bell. Dr. Bell amazed his students with his ability to diagnose patients by simply observing them. In addition to creating Sherlock Holmes, Conan Doyle also wrote *The Lost World*, which is credited as being the first fictional story to focus on dinosaurs.

Sir Arthur Conan Doyle was torn between his love of science and reason and his belief in spiritualism. He believed spirits from "the other world" could communicate with people on earth through mediums, people with special powers. He was even convinced that Houdini's escapes were due to amazing paranormal powers, despite Houdini's insistence that his escapes were all due to training and skill.

newspaper in which he said, "I have never seen or heard anything that could convince one there is a possibility of communication with the loved ones who have gone beyond." Sir Arthur was stung by Houdini's words, and their friendship began a rocky decline. Their exchanges became more public, as each wrote and responded to articles on spiritualism in major newspapers. "How long a private friendship can survive such an ordeal I do not know," Sir Arthur wrote to Houdini. The answer was "not long."

He did hope that people, particularly his mother, could communicate from the next world . . .

In 1924, Harry Houdini began touring the country not as an escape artist but as a lecturer about the tricks of phony mediums and the history of spiritualism. That spring Houdini also published *A Magician Among the Spirits*, in which he described the techniques used by some of the most famous mediums of the past and present. It also included a chapter on Sir Arthur Conan Doyle, which said that although Sir Arthur was a "brilliant man," he was blind in his acceptance of even fraudulent mediums. The book cost him a friendship. After the book was published, Sir Arthur never wrote to Harry again.

A poster promotes one of Houdini's performances, which exposed the techniques of spirit mediums. The performances combined some escape and magic tricks along with lecture and demonstrations.

The Scientific American Committee

In the same year, *Scientific American*, a science news magazine, offered two cash prizes to anyone who could produce a **psychic** photograph (one that showed beings from another world that was not manipulated by mechanical means) or a psychic **manifestation** of a physical nature (a phenomenon such as knocking, music, or others produced without trickery). The panel of judges included a Harvard University professor, an electrical engineer who had taught at the Massachusetts Institute of Technology, two psychic investigators, and Harry Houdini. The non-voting secretary was the associate editor of *Scientific American*.

Over the next two years, the committee tested several mediums, none of whom could pass. One challenger's powers,

A magazine features an illustration of a séance, including a spirit writing (center) and a flying guitar playing music. Séances became very popular in Europe and America in the early twentieth century.

though, nearly tore the committee apart. "Margery," as she was called to hide her true identity, was actually Mina Crandon, wife of a professor of surgery at Harvard Medical School. She and her husband only seemed interested in encouraging investigation of psychic phenomena, not in the prize money. The other members of the committee had already had several sittings with "Margery" before Houdini was told about her. They were all impressed and thought her psychic powers were real.

Uncovering Margery

Houdini attended his first séance with Margery in her home on a hot July night in Boston in 1924. Also attending were the publisher of *Scientific American* and two others from the committee. They sat in a circle, with Houdini sitting to Margery's

Houdini exposes the techniques of spirit mediums before a group at the Hippodrome in New York. He slips his foot from his shoe in order to ring a "spirit bell" beneath the table.

left and her husband to her right. They held hands and pressed their feet against one another to prove that the medium was not moving around whenever any effects took place. The lights were turned off. Soon the voice of Walter, Margery's dead older brother, was heard whispering and whistling around the room. After the lights were turned on so Margery could relax, a box with a bell inside was put on the floor near Houdini's feet. When the lights were turned off again, the bell inside the box rang and a megaphone was hurled through the air toward Houdini.

On the trip back to their hotel Houdini said, "I've got

Soon the voice of Walter, Margery's dead older brother, was heard whispering and whistling around the room.

her. All fraud, every bit of it. One more sitting and I'll expose everything." Earlier in the day he had worn a tight rubber surgical bandage around his lower right leg so that his skin would be swollen and sensitive to the touch of Margery's leg. He also rolled up his pant leg and could feel as Margery slowly moved her leg to

Houdini poses with Mina "Margery" Crandon and two members of the *Scientific American* committee investigating her, O.D. Munn (left) and J. Malcolm Bird (rear).

ring the bell. How did she throw the megaphone? That was easy, he said. Just as they turned off the lights, she quickly put it on top of her head, and when the time came she tipped her head toward Houdini to make it fall in his direction.

Another meeting had similar results. Walter insulted Houdini, the bell rang, and the card table around which they sat started shaking and rocking. Houdini felt certain he had uncovered Margery's methods. The other committee members were not convinced that she was a fake, though. They had to find a way to prove it one way or the other.

Houdini had an idea. He would build a wooden box in which Margery could sit in a chair, with only her head and arms sticking out. His woodworking assistant, Jim Collins, took Houdini's drawings and built the odd-looking box. The front sloped forward to allow for the top of the box to narrow near her head, but the lower part was broad enough to allow for her knees and legs as she sat in the chair.

In two more sessions with Houdini's box and a third with

Houdini demonstrates the box he designed to limit Mina Crandon's movements—and the ability of "spirits" to make their presence known. No spirits appeared during séances when she sat inside.

another device designed by another committee member, there were plenty of arguments and accusations, but no psychic signs occurred, except for the voice of "Walter" complaining of Houdini's shabby treatment of Margery. Before the third séance, the group had dinner together. Margery said she had heard Houdini planned to denounce her in public. She told him she did not want her son to hear his mother accused of being a fraud.

"Then don't be a fraud," Houdini replied.

In January 1925, Houdini appeared at Symphony Hall in Boston in January 1925 after the committee's preliminary report on Margery was published. It said that the committee was divided in their opinions about Margery, so the prize would not be awarded. He was now free to denounce Margery publicly.

During the evening he staged a séance with three volunteers who had their heads covered with hoods to simulate a darkened séance room. The rest of the audience got to watch in full light as Houdini re-created all of Margery's effects, including a demonstration from inside the same box he had built for her. He had finally found the right balance between his passions and his showmanship.

Later that year, Margery agreed to be tested by the psychology department at Harvard University. An article about their findings supported Harry's claims that she was a fraud. Houdini, a scrappy escape artist with little education, had outsmarted not only a clever trickster, but also a committee of men from some of the country's best universities.

Psychic Detectives

After the Margery case, Harry continued his investigations of other mediums. He developed a small group of psychic detectives who would travel in advance to the towns in which he was scheduled to speak. Sometimes Houdini would go undercover himself. In Cleveland, he wore old clothes and thick glasses to attend a séance with George Renner, a well-known medium. Houdini brought along a young companion who just happened to be a county prosecutor. During Renner's séances, trumpets floated in the air carrying the voices of people supposedly from the "other side." As soon as the lights went out for the séance to begin, Harry quickly rubbed black soot on the trumpets Renner had laid on the table. Voices soon were heard throughout the room. Suddenly Houdini turned on a flashlight. Renner's face and hands were covered in black from picking up the soot-covered instruments. Renner was arrested and tried for taking money under false pretenses.

Harry Houdini felt driven to uncover

Houdini holds bonds worth $10,000 in 1924. He offered them as a guarantee that he could repeat any spirit signs that occured during a séance led by Mina "Margery" Crandon.

Houdini's Number One Agent

The best and busiest of Houdini's psychic detectives was Rose Mackenberg, a Brooklyn-born woman who investigated, she estimated, three hundred mediums around the country. She would pretend to be a widow or a mother who had lost a child, or some other character she would invent.

Sometimes she even told mediums she wanted to become one herself. For a few dollars they would let her in on their secrets and give her a certificate making her a spiritualist minister. Houdini would tape together these "licenses" end-to-end and unfurl the resulting scroll before his audiences. She had so many of these papers that Houdini and her fellow agents called her "the Rev." Once she even bought the papers to own the Unity Spiritualist Church in Worcester, Massachusetts, for $13.50.

frauds who would take advantage of people's grief. Houdini understood about longing to speak again to a lost loved one. His campaign against dishonest mediums gave him more satisfaction than just about anything he had ever done in his life.

Houdini would often disguise himself when he went to investigate mediums. He used information that he and others gathered to uncover local frauds in towns around the country.

CHAPTER 11

Defying Death

I want my show to be the best of its kind whilst I am alive. When I am dead there will not be another like it.

In 1926, when Harry Houdini was fifty-two years old, a young man named Rahman Bey put on a show in New York with marvels to rival Houdini's. His act was the talk of the town. He claimed to be an Egyptian fakir, or holy man, suggesting his powers somehow were mystical. He pushed steel pins through his cheeks without showing any pain. He lay across a bed of nails. He even hypnotized animals.

Houdini was most upset when the young performer lay down in a coffin that was sealed shut and buried under sand. There Bey said he entered what he called a "cataleptic trance" and stayed for longer than eight minutes. How dare he! Houdini himself had done a similar "buried alive" stunt years before—without any help from phony trances. Despite his age, Houdini had to prove he was still the greatest.

"I guarantee to remain in any coffin that the fakir does for the same length of time he does, without going into any cataleptic trance."

Like Houdini, Bey was a master of publicity. With crowds and newspaper reporters gathered along the shoreline one July morning, Bey was to be sealed into a casket and lowered into the Hudson River. He was trying to stay underwater for an hour. While the casket was being lowered into the water, though, a bell placed inside—in case of emergency—went off. He was quickly returned to the pier. Although Bey claimed he had bumped the bell by accident, Houdini was ready to pounce. He issued a challenge in a New York newspaper: "I guarantee to remain in any coffin that the fakir does for the same length of time he does, without going into any cataleptic trance."

The Underwater Contest

Rahman Bey did not shrink from Houdini's challenge. In July, Bey had himself sealed into a casket that was lowered into a swimming pool. He remained underwater inside the casket, without any air being pumped in, for an hour.

Houdini's reputation was at stake. He had to take up the challenge. He began three weeks of furious, exhausting training, holding his breath for as long as possible and practicing staying very still and breathing quietly. He made his first attempt in secret in a glass-topped casket in the back room of the company that made it. The glass top allowed his assistants to see inside in case of an emergency and get him out quickly. Sweating and at times gasping for breath, he remained inside for an hour and ten minutes. Houdini was pleased, but he wondered whether some air might have seeped into the sealed casket.

When he made his second attempt a few days later, he made certain the casket was sealed so no air could enter. Then he had the casket lowered under a few inches of water so that he knew the seal was tight, but his assistants could still keep an eye on him. Again, he stayed inside for about an hour and ten minutes.

He was ready to make a public attempt. On August 5, 1926,

he was sealed into an iron casket and lowered into the swimming pool of the Hotel Shelton in New York. Houdini equipped the casket with a bell he could press in case of an emergency and a simple telephone wire through which he could speak with his assistant, Jim Collins, on the surface.

Collins called down to Houdini every few minutes to tell him how much time had passed. Houdini was sweating and panting by the time he had been underwater for an hour, but he kept on. When Collins called to say he had stayed there for an hour and twelve minutes, Houdini got his second wind. He

Workers prepare to lower a coffin containing Houdini into a hotel pool in 1926. Telephone wires emerging from the coffin allowed him to communicate with his assistant, Jim Collins, on the surface.

Houdini emerges from a casket after ninety minutes underwater at New York's Hotel Shelton. He smashed Rahman Bey's record of one hour underwater without added oxygen.

wanted to stay for at least fifteen minutes beyond the hour Bey had managed. The temperature inside was getting hotter and hotter. By then it had reached ninety-nine degrees, but he realized his feet were cooler than his head. He scrunched down toward the foot of the casket, and the cooler air there bought him a few more minutes inside. Soon, though, Houdini was having trouble breathing the tiny bit of air left and was becoming very sleepy, so he signaled to have the coffin raised to the surface. The Great Houdini had stayed underwater for an astonishing one hour and thirty minutes!

Houdini's Loyal Assistants

Houdini's assistants were a strong, talented, and, most important, loyal group of men who supported their boss in everything from

devising new escapes to helping serve at one of Bess's dinner parties. In 1910, Franz Kukol, the first of Houdini's assistants, was joined by Jim Collins, a talented carpenter and mechanic who was able to make Houdini's dazzling visions a reality. It was Collins who always tied Houdini's ropes before he was raised up to the top of buildings, and it was Collins who created the Chinese Water Torture Cell into which Houdini was lowered.

Houdini's loyal assistants and other close friends carry the escape artist's bronze coffin in his funeral procession on November 4, 1926.

Jim Vickery was the third of Houdini's closest assistants. Others came and went, but these three were part of Houdini's inner circle. Like anyone who sold Houdini an illusion or worked closely with him, they signed a pledge of secrecy. It read, in part:

"I do solemnly swear on my sacred honor as a man that as long as I live I shall never divulge the secret or secrets of Harry Houdini, or any thing I may make for him. . . . I further swear never to betray Houdini . . . so help me God almighty and may he keep me steadfast."

On Houdini's death, his assistants were pallbearers, carrying his heavy bronze casket to his final resting place.

Houdini's Final Days

As the escape master planned a new tour that fall, he had casket makers create a beautiful bronze casket to publicize the show—and to remind everyone that no one, especially not a phony Egyptian fakir, could beat Houdini. This time, though, he would be seeing how quickly he could escape from the casket, not how long he could stay inside. After he climbed inside it onstage, it was lowered into a glass box and buried under a ton of sand. The glass let the audience watch as Houdini escaped in a matter of minutes.

A poster promoting Houdini's tour after his underwater triumph over Egyptian fakir Rahman Bey. Houdini escaped onstage from a coffin buried under a ton of sand.

His tour was off to a great start. But during a performance in Albany, New York, something went wrong. While his assistants were raising him up by his ankles during the Upside Down, a trick he had been performing for years, he heard a snap and felt a sharp pain shoot up his left leg. His ankle was broken. Never one to let a little pain bother him, he had the foot bandaged up backstage and continued the show. He sat during some parts

The glass let the audience watch as Houdini escaped in a matter of minutes.

of his performances and wore a leg brace for the rest, but he continued his tour through New York State and then on to Montreal, Canada.

On the morning of October 22, 1926, Houdini lay on a small couch in his theater dressing room, resting his sore ankle as a McGill University student, Samuel Smilovitz, sketched him. The young artist and his friend, Jacques Price, were struck by how tired Houdini seemed.

In the early afternoon, another student named Whitehead joined the group. His first name remains a mystery. He asked Houdini questions on many topics, and he and Houdini talked for several minutes. Then Whitehead asked Houdini whether it was true that he could stand even the hardest blows to his abdomen, and wondered if he could try.

During the overnight train ride, the pain became too strong even for Houdini to bear.

Houdini agreed, but his broken ankle slowed him down as he tried to rise from the sofa. The young man started punching him before Houdini had a chance to stand and tighten his muscles. The other students were horrified at how hard Whitehead was hitting him. Houdini winced with each blow. The escape artist was in great pain.

Perhaps if Houdini had been less willing to work no matter how much pain he felt, he might have seen a doctor that day and saved his life. Instead, he performed his show that evening, resting backstage between acts. He still refused to see a doctor before he and Bess and their assistants boarded a train for Detroit. During the overnight train ride, the pain became too strong even for Houdini to bear. A doctor who was waiting to examine him when they arrived in Detroit was sure Houdini had appendicitis. The appendix is a finger-like pocket in the large intestine. When it becomes infected it can burst and spread poison throughout the body.

Despite the doctor's warning and a high temperature, Houdini insisted on performing that evening. He would not disappoint his opening-night audience. He collapsed backstage as soon as he finished his act. Doctors finally convinced Houdini to go to the hospital, where they removed his appendix. It had already burst, though, spreading infection throughout his body.

As days passed, the newspapers all carried updates on his condition, and flowers and telegrams flooded his hospital room. But the man who had defied death so many times before would

City officials and others surround Houdini's coffin on its arrival in New York for burial. Houdini died in Detroit on October 31, 1926.

Harry Houdini

April 6, 1874—October 31, (Hallowe'en) 1926

Mrs. Harry Houdini

"*Eyes of Memory Never Sleep*"

This memorial to Houdini, prepared by Bess, repeats Houdini's assertion that he had been born April 6, 1874, in Appleton, Wisconsin, rather than March 24, 1874, in Budapest, Hungary.

not be so lucky this time. Houdini died on Sunday, October 31, 1926, Halloween. The cause of death was infection caused by a burst appendix. The punches may have helped it burst when it did, but doctors believe the appendix would have burst eventually even without the blows.

Houdini's Funeral and Legacy

While Houdini lay in the hospital, his assistants packed up all his equipment to ship back to New York. One of the huge crates was lost in the warehouse and was not shipped. It contained the bronze casket that Houdini used for his "buried alive" trick. It was found in time to carry Houdini back home to New York. As he had requested, his head rested on a black bag filled with letters from his mother.

Approximately two thousand people attended his funeral in New York, including leaders in magic, theater, and journalism. Newspapers in big cities and small towns throughout the world carried stories about his death. Tributes to Houdini came from people everywhere, including Sir Arthur Conan Doyle, his old friend with whom he argued about spiritualism, and "Margery," the medium he had so publicly exposed.

Long before his death, Houdini set up a secret code with Bess and promised to contact her after he died if he could communicate from the "other world." Bess missed him terribly. Each Sunday, she sat in a room in their home in front of a photo of Houdini, waiting for some message. She even attended séances with mediums in the hope that he would speak to her, but he never did.

As Houdini had always said, his powers came from amazing skills, hard work, and secrets he took with him to the grave, not from any mystical powers. Years earlier Houdini wrote what may well be his own best tribute. He said, "I want my show to be the best of its kind whilst I am alive. When I am dead there will not be another like it."

Houdini had three clay busts of himself made. Two of them reportedly fell and smashed shortly after his death. This remaining statue resides at the Outagamie Museum in Appleton, Wisconsin.

Houdini's Burial Place

Houdini's brother Theo and his widow, Bess, visit Houdini's grave in 1928.

Harry Houdini was buried in a family plot at Machpelah Cemetery in Queens, New York, beside his beloved mother, Cecelia. Also buried there were his father, grandmother, and two brothers. Above the plots is a granite and marble bench. In Houdini's will, he requested that a bronze bust of himself that he had commissioned when he was in England be placed there.

The bust of Houdini no longer sits above the plot. Years after Houdini's death vandals removed it and damaged the site. Magician David Copperfield donated money to repair the destruction, but the bust was never replaced.

Hundreds of people still visit the plot each year. Some hope, perhaps, that he will speak to them from the grave. Others go simply to pay respects to one of the greatest showmen who ever lived.

Glossary

acrobats—performers who do gymnastic tricks such as back flips and cart-wheels to entertain.

anomalies—things that are strange or peculiar, hard to classify or identify.

automatons—machines that can perform tasks independently; robots.

biplane—an aircraft with two sets of wings, stacked one above the other.

confidant—a person who keeps another's secrets.

conjurer—a person who performs illusions; a magician.

contortionist—an acrobat who can twist his or her body into unusual shapes.

debunker—a person who exposes frauds or lies.

defier—one who challenges or fights the effects of something.

dummy—an imitation.

handcuffs—metal fasteners for wrists connected by chains or a bar.

imposter—a person who pretends to be someone else in order to deceive.

locksmiths—persons who make or repair locks.

manifestation—a demonstration as proof or evidence.

mediums—persons who claim to communicate between the earth and the spirit world.

metamorphosis—an abrupt change in appearance during development, as a caterpillar turns into a butterfly or a tadpole into a frog.

nom de plume—a false name used by an author; a pen name.

novelty act—a performance designed around an unusual talent, such as juggling or hypnosis.

playbills—flyers advertising performances or programs of performances.

psychiatric—related to the branch of medicine focusing on mental and behavioral disorders.

psychic—spiritual forces beyond the physical world.

regurgitate—to bring back up from the stomach to the mouth.

satirical—mockery used to expose vice or to poke fun at something.

séances—meetings where mediums try to contact the spirits of the dead.

shackles—metal bracelets usually attached to chains that confine the legs or arms.

sleight of hand—a trick that requires quick hand movements.

soft-pedaled—played down to make less visible or obvious.

straitjacket—a garment of strong material designed to bind the arms tightly to restrain the wearer.

trapeze—a piece of equipment like a swing suspended high above the ground used by performers.

Bibliography

Brandon, Ruth. *The Life and Many Deaths of Harry Houdini*. New York: Random House, 1993.

Christopher, Milbourne. *Houdini: The Untold Story*. New York: Thomas Y. Crowell Company, 1969.

Gibson, Walter B. *The Original Houdini Scrapbook*. New York: Corwin Sterling, 1976.

Gresham, William Lindsay. *Houdini: The Man Who Walked Through Walls*. New York: Henry Holt, 1959.

Henning, Doug. *Houdini: His Legend and His Magic*. New York: Time-Life Books, 1991.

Houdini, Harry. *A Magician Among the Spirits*. Alexandria, Virginia: Times Books, 1977.

Kellock, Harold. *Houdini: His Life Story by Harold Kellock from the Recollections and Documents of Beatrice Houdini*. New York: Harcourt, Brace & Company, 1928.

Silverman, Kenneth. *Houdini!!!: The Career of Ehrich Weiss*. New York: Harper Collins, 1996.

Image Credits

About the Author

Rita Thievon Mullin lives in Fairfax, Virginia. She is the author of *Thomas Jefferson*, also in this series, and of *Animalogy* and *Who's for Dinner?* When not writing books for children, she works in program development for a cable television channel.

Index